EACH HUMAN SPIRIT

THE TRANSFORMATION OF THE
AMERICAN WORKPLACE

*"The workplace has failed to develop the most
diverse renewable resource in America…
the human spirit."*

ART BOBROWITZ

Opal Creek
P r e s s

Opal Creek Press, LLC
1630 Saginaw St. S.
Salem, OR 97302
www.opalcreekpress.com

We gratefully acknowledge the following for permission to quote previously published material:
Leadership and The New Science; Learning About Organization From an Orderly Universe, copyright 1992 by Margaret Wheatley, Berrett-Koehler Publishers, Inc., San Francisco, CA. All rights reserved. 1.800.929.2929.
The Economics of Trust: Liberating Profits and Restoring Corporate Vitality, copyright 1996, by John Whitney, McGraw-Hill Companies.
The Manager's Book of Quotations, copyright 1989, by Lewis D. Eigen and Jonathan P. Siegel, The Quotation Corporation, AMACOM, a division of American Management Association International, New York. All rights reserved.

Due to space constraints, portions of the Acknowledgements and the Citations pages also reflect permission to quote or reprint.

Manufactured in the United States of America
Cover design: Bruce DeRoos, Portland, Oregon
Author photograph by: Vincent Zollner Photography, Salem, Oregon
Layout: Paradigm Graphics, Salem, Oregon
Opal Creek Press and the Opal Creek Press logo are trademarks belonging to Opal Creek Press, LLC.

Library of Congress Cataloging-in-Publication Data

Bobrowitz, Art, 1946-

Each human spirit: b the transformation of the American workplace / Art Bobrowitz.

      p. cm.
Includes index.
ISBN 1-931105-03-0
1. Industrial management—United States. 2. Organizational effectiveness—United States. 3. Management—Employee participation—United States. I. Title.
HD70.U5 B63 2001
658.3—dc21
      2001000799

To my students—
who taught me.

CONTENTS

ACKNOWLEDGEMENTS

I want to thank my wife, Roseann, who is my soul mate and best friend. I would not have been able to write this book if it weren't for her nudges of support and her insightful comments. She gracefully tolerated the many times I rose at 4:00 AM to write and the difficult process of endless revision. She supported this project heart and soul, and I would not have been able to complete it without her.

The final product would not have happened without the guidance and vision of Kristi Negri from Opal Creek Press. It becomes a challenge when you have something to say on leadership and management, but must become a student of the process of saying it. Kristi's talents brought my project from a series of table-thumping thoughts to a finished document on change. She has the rare gift of understanding one's visions and dreams and turning them into a manuscript.

I also want to thank four individuals who gave me permission to share their stories or wisdom in these pages. They are: Frank Krecji, inspirational leader and furniture manufacturer; Margaret Wheatley, who opened new territory in organizational science; Senator Bob Bennett, who in his book with Kurt Hanks and Gerreld L. Pulsipher, *Gaining Control*, explained the concept of belief windows; Pastor Morris Dirks, who automatically answered my questions about the workplace in spiritual terms.

I also thank God for the splendid woods by Mt. Zion Cemetery in Brookfield, Wisconsin. It was there as a child that my father taught me how trees and plants work together for growth and harmony. It was my first lesson in organizational change.

Preface

A Call to a New View

I make my living as a trainer, speaker and management consultant. I've been doing this in one capacity or another for more than twenty-seven years and have had the opportunity to get an insider's view of a number of corporations and governmental agencies. What I've seen has often dismayed me. It's hard to believe what people do to people in the name of "good business." We have developed a culture where sometimes appalling attitudes toward others are accepted and even touted as everyday business practice. I have been fortunate, however, to also spend time in businesses that are redefining the rules of what a good business can be.

It is the leaders of these good businesses who have inspired me to write this book. I have found in these people, individuals who are not afraid to look at things in new ways. They are redefining what it means to be successful in business beyond a transient figure on the bottom line. Yet these people are not ignoring the bottom line. Theirs are profit-based businesses or results-oriented organizations. They have simply figured out a new approach, a new definition of good business. It is my attempt to quantify this approach that I offer to you in the pages that follow.

When I first began to observe these new organizations, I quickly realized that I would need to create a vocabulary to describe them. Traditional management terms and approaches simply don't communicate the essence of what I've seen. The word I finally determined to be at the core of this new approach to business might come as a shock. The word is *spiritual.* The essential challenge of the American workplace is not productivity or a lack of manpower or the fluctuations in this market or that. It is the state of the heart and soul of the American worker.

I should explain that I come from a strong Christian tradition. My personal faith and what I wish for others in terms of spiritual fulfillment is central to my life. It is perhaps this basis that led me to view this management revolution in a spiritual context. But if I take my personal beliefs away and stick to the definitions and viewpoint I created, the model still makes sense. This work is not the result of dogma, nor does it require a spiritual viewpoint close to my own for the labels to stick. I simply state that the key to a productive and successful workforce in this nation is leadership's ability to recognize the spiritual nature of the American worker and to nurture that spirit in order to harness the full potential available to us as a society.

With this book I issue a challenge. I don't ask that you necessarily agree with my conclusions. I merely ask that you take an honest look at the workplace from this altered perspective and evaluate how it looks to you.

We can continue to travel down the road of increased labor litigation, declining product quality and ballooning legislation. Or, we can come to recognize that the heart and soul of the American worker needs to be expressed and cannot be legislated into conformity. The human spirit needs nurturing just as the body requires nourishment. It cannot be delegated, substituted, pacified, or hidden behind the veil of political correctness.

This book is not about feeling good or ignoring the business of business. It is about a change of viewpoint only and the implications of that change. It is about the recognition that despite any personal credo or religious background, there is a spiritual aspect to each of us. Both Eastern and Judeo-Christian traditions teach that we are spiritual beings. We are all connected, we all have value, and we are all striving in our own way to find our best path. It simply doesn't make sense for us to expect people to devote such a large part of their life energy to the workplace and ignore this reality.

This evidence of the human spirit in the workplace can be something we fight or integrate. It can be something we stifle or nurture. I believe the revolution is already under way. The old autocratic styles of management are quickly becoming unacceptable to the workforce. We need only look at the intensity of our labor disputes and labor-initiated court cases to see what's happening. We have to change. As our society changes to embrace the spiritual aspect of the workplace, the ability for a company or organization to survive might well hinge on its ability to adapt to a more spirit-based model. But this is more than just about survival. It is about doing what is right in America. It is time to address this issue of the human spirit, of each human spirit.

THE NEED FOR THE HUMAN SPIRIT TO WORK

IS AS GREAT AS THE BODY'S NEED TO BREATHE.

OUR SOULS ARE NURTURED BY OUR HANDS AND HEARTS.

THE SEVEN NEEDS FOR PERSONAL PRODUCTIVITY

"One of the greatest diseases is to be nobody to anybody."

Agnes Gonxha Bojaxhiu (Mother Teresa)
Roman Catholic nun and humanitarian

I n my twenty-seven years of teaching and working with employees, I have spent countless hours listening to them talk about their jobs and careers. At first, I regarded the information they passed on to me as either personal stories or expressions of frustration. I listened, but I didn't realize what these people were really telling me. Over time, however, a pattern emerged and I began to ask specific questions. The study I did was not scientific, it was simply asking people what about their jobs gave them satisfaction and what they wanted from their work. As I sifted and categorized these responses, I came up with seven basic needs for job fulfillment. I began to observe the effects of having these needs fulfilled—or not fulfilled—and I realized how closely these seven needs are linked to productivity.

What I learned from my students was that productivity is much more than an external manifestation of energy and output. It's more than having the right tool at hand at the right place at the right time. In fact, I believe that productivity has less to do with the scientific side of production management than it does the spiritual and personal growth of the individual.

Let me say that again: *I believe that productivity has less to do with the scientific side of production management, than it does the spiritual and personal growth of the individual.*

To a manager who is more comfortable crunching numbers and analyzing efficiency, that last statement will be profoundly threatening. After all, isn't it enough that we have to pay wages, benefits, and provide a safe and clean, harassment-free workplace? My belief is that it is *not* enough.

Every worker needs certain things from his or her job. This is true whether we are talking about leaders, managers, or front-line employees. These needs are as basic as the air we breathe and the food we eat. If we want our employees to invest in our company goals, and hence boost productivity, we must first invest in meeting the seven basic workplace needs of our employees.

It's easier than it sounds. It is simply a matter of rethinking the issues.

Unfortunately, rethinking the issues runs against the corporate conditioning of the modern American workplace. Out of fear, we have slowly bargained away the spiritual and personal commitment of our employees. Most managers have learned to focus on keeping the company out of the judicial system. While one can easily understand how this attitude developed, it doesn't replace leadership. It's impossible to lead a company forward from a defensive posture. In fact, I believe that the most costly product manufactured in America isn't even a line item in the budget. It is downstream thinking and cover-your-butt management.

But the managers aren't the only ones affected. Employees today are afraid to commit to an idea, principle, concept or project, because they sense no commitment or loyalty on behalf of the company. Employees mentally run every idea through an external, politically correct, socio-political filter and find that nothing is worth the risk or effort. If their ideas aren't solicited or even welcomed, there is little reward in offering them. This loss of creativity and potential is as expensive as the lack of leadership.

Everyone seems to be running scared. Employees don't trust the company, and the company doesn't trust the employees. No wonder we have problems in the workplace!

How do we turn this around? As with all great movements in history, it begins with individuals having the courage to change their own course. Individuals change, then companies change, and then the broader corporate culture changes. If we learn to rethink how we look at our jobs, our employees, and our organizations, we can put trust and loyalty back into the workplace.

Without it, we can only expect increased litigation, costly labor negotiations, and diminishing product quality. And, worse yet, more people will hate their jobs and live without the fulfillment they might otherwise enjoy.

The Seven Needs For Personal Productivity

I believe in these seven needs. No one need is more important than another; they are all powerful. It took me a long time to identify and label these needs, but once I did, I recognized them consistently in my students, my clients, and in myself. I saw how considering these needs can change one's life.

Also, I saw that creating a positive environment where these needs can be reliably met requires both the employees and the leadership. No doubt, both groups can always find something lacking in the other side, and finger pointing is an effective way of avoiding our own responsibilities. What I challenge you to do is to read these comments with a spirit of self-examination. You can't control what the other side does, but you can control your own choices. Here are the seven needs:

1. Your work must have meaning.

What you do for a living must be tied into a greater sense and purpose. Your work must be connected to your principles, values and ethics. I describe this as the spiritual connection one has with his or her career. This doesn't mean that you must immediately stop what you are doing and embark on a strictly humanitarian path, but it does mean that you need to be able to connect in some way to the goals and mission of the organization in which you work. You must be able to identify with it in some way that appeals to your greater self. If your company makes the best widgets in the world, then you can take pride in helping to deliver those widgets. If, on the other hand, you despise the company, find that the goals and intentions are not in line with your personal views, you can collect all the paychecks you want, but you are growing steadily poorer.

Here is where leadership becomes so important.

If the leadership is not communicating a defined set of values and goals, the employees cannot find a worthwhile connection to the company. Productivity can only suffer as a result.

In a company where leadership communicates a mission and ethic, you find people who clearly love their work. They see their work as important and worthwhile. Their own contribution might be relatively small, but it is never insignificant because it applies to a greater whole in which they take pride.

Our work should be a form of spiritual fulfillment. It is a daily expression of our relationship with the world and, I believe, our relationship to God. Learning what it takes to add this dimension of meaning to your life is not always easy. While leadership has a role in the equation, it is only half the story. Leadership can offer meaning, but the employees have to be willing and able to connect to it.

Sometimes, to be able to connect, you have to take a careful inventory of what is stored inside your personal warehouse. As Max Weber, the nineteenth-century sociologist stated, "…the individual is the upper limit and sole carrier of meaningful conduct." If we take count of what is in our warehouse, then we must also become accountable.

We might find that we are missing something in our personal warehouse. Or, we might find that we have so much old baggage stored in there that we can't find the real valuables. Clearing out the warehouse can be painful and time-consuming, but if we don't have a meaningful connection to our life work, taking inventory is the first step in finding out why.

2. You must have input into your destiny.

Every employee would like to have complete control over his or her destiny in an organization, but that is not realistic. You do, however, want to be listened to and have your ideas and thoughts received with interest and respect. It is simply the right to speak your mind and voice your beliefs.

There are several dysfunctional management styles that send the message to employees to "shut up, put up, and get to work." Sometimes this is an unspoken message, but it is surprising how often you can hear almost those exact words come from a manager. If the leadership is going to perpetuate, or at least tolerate, this type of atmosphere, they really can't be surprised when they run up against labor problems and poor productivity. They get what they ask for—no creativity, no loyalty, and no employee investment in the output.

Sometimes management will offer the defense that the suggestion box is always available. The goal is not a lot of suggestions in the suggestion box. If a healthy employee-management dialogue exists, people will be talking and the suggestion box will be empty.

This is not to say that every idea that issues from somebody's mouth must immediately be implemented. If an employee has an egocentric view of the world, no amount of open-door management is going to enable that person to find fulfillment in the workplace. But management must take a serious look at how ideas are generated in the organization. What mechanisms exist to enable every voice to be heard? How are unsolicited suggestions treated?

And, employees must be willing to look at the larger picture. They must be willing to see what factors beyond their daily experience might have an effect on whether their ideas could, or even should, be implemented.

3. You must be paid a fair wage.

When I asked my students to talk about salaries, it's surprising how often they talked about something else. They all acknowledged that it is important to have their bills paid and to be financially comfortable. And, most conceded that it would be nice to be wealthy, but the amount of money most people cited that would make them feel wealthy was often a surprisingly modest amount. Why is this?

It has long been established that money is not a long-term motivator in the workplace. If you doubt this, ask yourself these questions: "If my boss walked in today and said my salary was going to be doubled, would I immediately start to work twice as hard? If I did work harder, how long would the incentive last? What would I be willing to give up out of my twenty-four hours each day to double my salary? Time with my family? Sleep? Relaxation activities?" If you're like most people, you quickly realize that while you need a certain amount of money to function comfortably in our society, the real compensation in the workplace is more than dollars and cents.

Clearly, having the other six workplace needs met is at the core of what makes us happy in our employment, but compensation is important. Let's look at other aspects of compensation that don't come through the company benefits program.

Recently, I called on a client who was interested in some employee training. While I was waiting for my appointment, I couldn't help but notice the front desk attendant. When the phone rang she answered it with a great attitude and took personal responsibility for directing the call. As people came to her desk, she made positive eye contact and showed a genuine concern for what she did.

When I was leaving the office I walked up to her and told her I was impressed by her attitude and complimented her on her demeanor. She thanked me and said she loved her job. I was impressed by her sense of pride. She was a temporary fill-in from a job placement service and was probably getting entry-level pay.

She didn't have a lot of status, nor was she making much money, but what a world of experience was at her feet. She was taking in everything she could. She was getting paid a fair wage because what she was learning would be instrumental in her next position. By keeping her eyes open and absorbing everything she could each day, she was increasing her own compensation. It is certain she wouldn't be making entry-level wages for long.

Another non-benefit form of compensation is a mentor in the organization who is willing to guide you. Such a person can provide you with invaluable knowledge and can serve as an advocate for you. Perhaps more importantly, a mentor can show you by example, how to be a leader. With the guidance of a mentor, you can avoid many of the pitfalls that might otherwise become barriers to achieving your goals. Not everyone finds a mentor, but if you are fortunate to have one, don't underestimate the value of that relationship.

A less direct form of mentorship is the presence of enlightened leadership. Working for a true leader is a marvelous opportunity for personal growth. Watch how your leaders lead. Choose the qualities in them you want to emulate and practice them while you are in an environment you know supports these values. Leaders lead at the level at which they find themselves. It is never too soon to start building leadership muscles.

Employees must look at their entire employment picture when determining if they are being paid a fair wage. If the wage at your present job is lower than it might be elsewhere, yet you are preparing yourself for more success, perhaps faster, down the road, which job is really giving you the best compensation? A fair wage can be comprised of many things.

It is easy to fixate on money. It's measurable. It's easy to compare the money at Company A with the money at Company B, but we must be careful to keep the intangible compensation in sight if we want to be fulfilled in the workplace.

The ability to meet the other six of the seven needs, the opportunity for experience and education, and the presence of a mentor or inspired leader must find a place in our calculations if we are to consider a fair wage.

4. Your work must add quality to your life.

To add to your quality of life, your job must do more than pay the bills. Your work must charge your battery and energize you to relate to and enjoy the time you are away from it. This is true whether you're the president of a corporation or a dishwasher at the corner café. Your job is meeting your need for quality of life if you find yourself looking forward to going to work in the morning, and at the same time, you have enthusiasm for your time away from it.

Ask yourself: How does your job affect your sleep? Do you awaken refreshed or are you full of dread, anxiously solving problems the instant you open your eyes?

While it is reasonable to expect that you need to give your job your best efforts every day, is your job taking all the best effort you have? If you consistently leave your job at the end of the day and don't have the energy or emotional resources to be with your family or do whatever else you hope to do with your free time, you need to pay attention to that.

We don't get to save time. We might become more efficient with the time we have, but we don't get bonus time. If you had wanted to spend two hours at your child's softball game today, and didn't, you don't get that back. If you had wanted a couple of hours in the evening to read a book to refresh yourself and instead you stayed late at the office, that opportunity is gone forever.

Today is not a rehearsal for a better day. It's all we've got.

I think one of the problems we face in our over-litigated society is that we habitually look outside ourselves for the origins of our problems. When we've failed at our day, we blame work, our boss, our family, the bills, the dog, or anyone else we think is making us feel bad. Our challenge is to realize that each day is a series of events. From brushing our teeth in the morning, to shopping for a new pair of shoes, to talking on the telephone, every small way we spend our time is defining who we are. The trick is to decide which of these events we can control and which we cannot.

Of course, it can be overwhelming to consider scrutinizing each action all through the day, but consider this:

If you look at your twenty-four hours and decide that You Are Your Job, and that definition of yourself is not one you like, you need to stand back and take a look at your choices.

We all have choices. Sometimes we just need to uncover what our choices might really be.

There are people who have figured this out. Their work and personal lives blend in such a way that it's almost difficult to see where one ends and the other begins. Their work is a part of them that makes them feel good about themselves and the world in which they live. They are their work—and they are many other things besides. Their work leaves them with enthusiasm for the things that keep them in balance, whether that be family, their faith, hobbies, or quiet relaxation. Every one of us can strive for this ideal through the choices we make daily. Quality of life is not a destination. It is a journey.

While the burden of meeting this fourth need for quality of life is ultimately on the individual, it is important for our workforce leadership to recognize this need and come to terms with what it means for management expectations on the workforce. Does management look at the workforce as drones to drive to the limit, or does it see employees as twenty-four hour people who happen to spend a large portion of their available time at work? Is it possible that giving an employee the opportunity to go to his or her child's softball game might result in increased productivity down the road? Are employees going home at the end of the day with a sense of accomplishment for a day well spent or are they filled with anxiety and stress? It is easy to rationalize any kind of answer to these questions, and our tendency is to do so.

The real question for leadership is: Apart from the salary, does this organization contribute to the quality of life of its workers? If the job gives employees no opportunity to keep their lives balanced, there is a problem with balance in the organization, and eventually, the organization will pay the price. *This is not to discourage hard work and high expectations, or even long hours.* It is simply to suggest that each human spirit needs to live life in a balanced way with mind, body, and spirit. At some level, we all know this, and our ability to work toward that balance is a basic need for personal productivity.

5. Your work must bring meaningful relationships to your life.

In my interactions with employees, I repeatedly hear how

important it is for people to encounter, work with, and grow professionally with a peer group. Employees interact at many levels.
If the organization fosters a team spirit, as opposed to one of internal competition, the workplace is welcoming instead of threatening. There will be more communication, more sharing of talents and ideas, and more emotional support. This can only boost
productivity.

In my view, workplace relationships are more than social
structures or, as in the case of team organization and formal
mentoring, sound business practice. I believe that the true need
being met in workplace relationships is a spiritual one. Our peer
relationships make us grow. They challenge our belief systems or
reinforce them. They keep us in touch with our twenty-four hour
reality. We can feel that our workplace experiences are shared
and understood. It is important that we are not grinding away in
isolation. Peer relationships nourish us, and in cases where they
extend outside the workplace, they can enhance our personal lives
as well.

These relationships can also help us determine whether our
other basic needs are being met. For example, if we work with a
group of people who all believe in the mission of the organization, it validates our own sense of meaning in our job. If the work
itself does not sustain us, it could be the personal support and
social interaction that does.

All of this is not to say that management must tolerate

excessive development of meaningful peer relationships without sacrificing the profit margin to chit-chat time. What I am advocating is a realization of this basic need in our workers and the creation of an environment that promotes the workplace bond by enhancing communication and team efforts.

A library-type atmosphere with patrolling enforcers will perhaps get the work done, but the organization will not flourish. Management won't get any pleasant surprises on the productivity side of things, and it will have eliminated the potential for truly exciting innovation to occur. The synergism of involved, supported intellects cannot be underestimated. It is good for the company, and it makes for a fulfilling workplace.

6. Your work must provide variety in what you do.

I use the word "variety" to describe this need, because meeting this need does not necessarily mean doing many different things. If a person is doing a repetitive task, but sees the value in the task and takes pride in doing the task well, he or she doesn't necessarily need to be shifted to another job to get variety. It might be that she assumes a leadership role in her area and that function meets the need for variety, or it might be that he continually learns more about the larger picture, formally or informally, and that his new knowledge provides the variety he needs.

For most workers, though, if the job doesn't hold variety or some other educational value, it is important to cross train or job share. Someone who is bored can't possibly look forward to going to work in the morning. People who feel like a cog in an impersonal wheel cannot find meaning in their work. Ultimately, the job won't add quality to their lives.

The workplace must broaden our horizons. This can be done by investing in training for every level of the organization. Looking at things in new ways or learning new techniques is one way to fill the need for variety. Sometimes simply doing a different physical task for awhile helps. In the case of cross-training, it also helps the organization. Variety nourishes the mind, which eventually feeds the spirit. Any time the human spirit is nourished, we all reap the benefits.

7. Your work must be viewed as important.

Management knows every job is important. If a job weren't important, it would be cut in the budgeting process. Why then, is it so hard sometimes for management to pass that acknowledgment, that a function is *necessary*, along to the person who is performing it?

This need is different from the first need, that the work must have meaning. The need for meaning is what people take to every career move they make. It is a philosophical and theological connection. The need for number seven, to know that the work is viewed as important, is specific to the individual workplace. It speaks to the relationship the employer creates with the employee.

If employees know that what they do is important for the organization, they have the opportunity to take pride in their job. I like to think of Albert Einstein and his idea that time to one individual is different as it relates to another. The same is true of job importance. It is relative to the individual's identity and connection with the organization. If an individual in a specific function knows that the organization values that function, no matter where it fits into the picture, the employee's need can be met and the potential for increased productivity is enhanced.

Of course, some people are able to look around themselves and find the value in their roles without it being clearly defined for them. They innately know how they fit into the organization and why what they do matters. They don't need as much external validation about their roles as others might.

Sometimes this is related to function. An attorney who is winning cases for clients sees daily that his or her work is important to others. You don't have to look far, though, to find roles where the effect of the work is not so evident. The person sweeping the shop floor alone in the middle of the night or the valet parking cars needs to know that his or her function is an important part of the larger picture.

A REALITY CHECK

Having stated these needs in general terms, I think it's important to point out that there are people out there who won't respond in the ways I've described. I believe them to be a small minority, but nevertheless, they exist. No matter what the organization might do, these folks will never fit into the organization and, in fact, I wonder if they have any intention of fitting into the organization from the start.

It would probably take a psychoanalyst to explain why these people don't seem to have the same responses in an organizational setting that most of us have, but given that they exist, for whatever reason, let's take a look at how the workplace adapts in negative ways to their presence.

I would guess that most managers who have read this chapter to this point stopped at a few points along the way and thought of one or more individuals they've encountered in the past who blew my theories out of the water. I can hear the internal voice now: "Art Bobrowitz never ran into (you fill in the name.)" Fact is, I have. What I question is our remodeling of corporate America in defense against a few individuals.

We make policies from a defensive posture, and we fear giving an inch to our employees in case some individual will subsequently try to take a mile. These are valid fears, and they are the realities of our workplace. The challenge for employers and employees both, then, is to look at the situation clearly and choose to nourish the human spirit in every way we can within the constraints we have.

Management, you have a responsibility to sift those constraints carefully. Which are truly necessary and which are just an excuse to do things the easy way? We owe it to ourselves, to the twenty-four hour people who work for us, and to our society, to be and become forces for quality in life, not destroyers.

Employees, you also have responsibility. First, you must take responsibility for your own happiness. This is hard to do, but goes to the root of the problem. We must stop looking at management as a scapegoat for all that is going wrong with our lives. What can you change? What can't you change? Figure that out and you are on your way. Secondly, you have a responsibility to try to see the view from the management side. What are their goals? What are their fears? Are they not twenty-four hour people, too? In exchange for your paycheck and benefits and any of the intangible compensations of your workplace, what do you owe your employer? Are you honoring your end of the contract?

A New Vocabulary

We aren't accustomed to talking about management goals, productivity, or employer/employee relationships in terms of the human spirit, but once we realize that the human spirit is what drives everything else, a spirit-based vocabulary makes complete sense in the workplace.

Recognizing that, I decided to seek out some of the spiritual leaders in my community and see what they had to say on this issue. Several people suggested that I see Pastor Morris Dirks of the Christian Missionary Alliance Church in Salem, Oregon. His congregation is very active and involved in many aspects of the community. I asked Pastor Dirks, "If you could take the pulse of the working people of your congregation, what are three things they are sick of in the workplace?" It didn't surprise me when his answer could have been taken straight from the list of Seven Needs. Here is what he said troubled people in the workplace:

- Their inability to connect meaningfully to the organization. Their work lacks a spiritual sense of purpose or destiny.
- Seeing their work and the tasks they perform as pointless.
- Not having the authority to change their world.

My next question was, "If you could tell the members of your congregation three things to help them survive the workplace in America, what would they be?" He replied:

- Look for the Kingdom of God in everything you do. Find the spirit of God in your work.
- Find the calling behind the calling in your life.
- Your employer is not your master. You are working for the Glory of God.

I loved his answer, because it unabashedly addressed the needs of the workplace in spiritual terms.

Our belief in God, however we characterize that belief, and our commitment to our life calling is our true motivator, whether we acknowledge it or not.

I believe the concerns about the workplace I've been hearing from employees for all these years really boil down to them searching for a universal statement of self-respect, dignity and a longing for a sense of completeness.

Their workplace concerns are *essentially spiritual*, and we keep trying to make them about something else.

The rules of St. Benedict say, "Work is prayer and prayer is work." When we begin to view our workplace in a spiritual context, however we define that spirituality, we change our expectations and behaviors accordingly. Our entire relationship to work and to our co-workers changes. It is then that we have the opportunity to maximize personal productivity both for our own benefit and for the benefit of the organizations we serve.

How to Use the Seven Needs for Career Change

Once people recognize the seven needs, the inevitable question is, "What if my seven needs aren't being met?" Of course, it doesn't take a huge leap of intellect to figure out that it is unrealistic to find any company that meets all seven needs for every employee. Therefore, it isn't practical to jump ship if an organization fails at meeting some number of these needs. So the question becomes, "How many of the seven needs can go unmet before a career change is in order?"

In observing people and getting feedback from my students,

I decided that if you take a good look at your situation and four of the seven needs aren't being met over time, it's probably good to think about a move.

Of course, deciding to leave an unsatisfying job is just one part of finding fulfillment in the workplace. You also need to find a new situation where you have a chance of having more of the seven needs met. The ideal interviewing situation allows you to meet with staff as well as the interviewer. If you get this opportunity, and perhaps you should consider asking for it if it isn't offered, think about questions you might ask that give you insight into each of the seven needs. Consider these:

1. Your work must have meaning. "Are employees able to see a connection between the work they do and the organization's mission statement?"

2. You must have input into your destiny. "How do employees communicate with management? Do employees have an opportunity to provide input and are their ideas considered ?"

3. You must be paid a fair wage. "How do the wages and benefits compare with similar organizations?" What non-monetary benefits do you see in this job? What opportunities are there for personal growth and advancement?"

4. Your work must add quality to your life. "Is the organization supportive of employees as people who have families and lives outside the job?"

5. Your work must bring meaningful relationships to your life. "Does the corporate structure support mentoring, either formally or informally? Do employees tend to build positive cooperative relationships with team and/or department members?"

6. Your work must provide variety in what you do. "What kind of opportunities are there for professional growth? Does the company hire from within, cross train, provide formal training or other forms of education?"

7. Your work must be viewed as important. "Do the employees have a sense that they are important to the organization and that their work is recognized? How does that occur?"

IN CONCLUSION

We have arrived at our current situation, where the loyalty between employer and employee sometimes seems to be non-existent, not through some accident of fate, but as a result of the attitudes which immediately preceded us in the workplace.

It is time we evaluate our relationships to the workplace in terms of human fulfillment, the spiritual function that work performs in our lives. When we understand that and learn to address the needs of the human spirit in the workplace, productivity will soar at both the individual and the organizational levels.

COMPANY HEADQUARTERS SHOULD NOT BE A

COLLECTION OF BRILLIANT MINDS FOCUSED ON FUNCTION.

IT SHOULD BE AN ASSEMBLY OF HONEST PEOPLE

COMMITTED TO THE WELFARE OF THE HUMAN SPIRIT

AND THE COMMON GOOD.

A WALK IN THE WOODS

*"The lion tamer school of management: Keep them well fed and
never let them know that all you've got is a chair and a whip."*

Anonymous

I have childhood memories of walking in the woods near my
Wisconsin home. I loved to think about what it would be
like to live in the wilderness as the early settlers did. Any
time I was out of sight of a house or building, I pretended I was
blazing new trails on the edge of the frontier.

As I've grown, I've discovered that a walk in the woods still
sets me to thinking, except the frontiers I find myself thinking
about have changed. Instead of settlers and log cabins, the woods
now remind me of how organizations could be if we only had the
courage to make them so.

When you look at the woods, what do you see? Is it a mass of
randomly growing vegetation, everything fighting for sunlight,
trying to edge out the next guy? Are the downed trees cluttering
up the forest floor and contributing to a chaos that could be man-

aged if humans would just step in and clean it up? Or, do you see the forest as a highly organized statement of nature, where the tall trees shelter the underlying vegetation from a sun too harsh? Are the different species working in conjunction for mutual benefit? Are the fallen trees a source of nutrients for future growth?

If we look at the forest in a traditional sense, I think it looks like chaos. If we look at it as a naturalist would, however, we would be astounded by the order and intricacy of what we see. What opportunities we miss by looking at something from only one perspective.

To me, the forest is the perfect metaphor for looking at our organizations. What would happen if we tried to box up the forest and enforce order upon it? Would there still be the diversity of plants and animals? Would the ecosystem remain healthy and self-renewing? What do we lose if we make a forest look like an organization? My guess is that imposing too much structure on the forest kills it, or at least kills elements of it. We need to ask ourselves about the structures we impose on our employees. Are we strangling creativity and making it impossible for ideas to bloom? Are only the tallest and straightest trees valuable? Are we looking for a forest we can harvest today, or one we can maintain indefinitely?

I've often wondered what might happen if a management team started holding their meetings in the woods. How would the management team in your organization respond if you took them to the woods, asked them to look around and then answer these questions?

- *How does this natural environment work together?*
  Is there a correlation in our company? How do different departments/people/groups work together?

- *What are the different elements of the forest?*
  What are the corresponding elements in our organization?

- *What does it take to nourish this forest?*
  What does it take to nourish our organization? Is that nourishment freely given so that our organization thrives, or are our people subject to drought and a harsh environment?

- *Pick out an individual plant, tree, or animal. What would cause it to die?*
  What would cause the corresponding element in our organization to fail?

- *How does nature renew itself?*
  How does our organization renew itself? Are we interfering with the renewal process in our organization by trying to control too much?

It is human nature to want to organize what is disorganized. We train ourselves from infancy to pick up the mess, put things in order, and get with the system. But if we can't set that training aside sometimes, we are destined to always see chaos in the forest, or in our lives, or in our organizations; where in reality there might be an elegant system in place that we are simply not seeing.

I believe it's time for a new perspective in the management of organizations. We need to look more closely at what might appear to be chaos in the organization and be sure we are not (forgive the pun) missing the forest for the trees.

I'm not the first to be fascinated by this idea of order in apparent chaos. Margaret Wheatley describes this concept brilliantly in her book, *Leadership and the New Science: Learning about Organization from an Orderly Universe.* Her correlation between quantum mechanics and the way organizations can work really struck home with me, because for me, the forest speaks of the order and necessity of chaos.

I would like to tell you the story of the ABC Millwork Company. I have changed the name of the company, but the story is true. This was a company with the best of intentions and a management team that had it all wrong. *It is the story of what happens when you don't manage the forest properly.* It is also a story of renewal.

A young man with a dream and an ability to make things happen founded ABC Millwork. He started his woodworking business in a small shop with two other carpenters. After time, he hired more personnel and with hard work, started to make the company grow. This man hired good people. Things were going well, but what happened next almost led to his undoing. He needed to hire managers, so thinking that "if you can't trust your friends, who can you trust?" he hired his friends and put them in management positions. *If you are going to manage the forest, make sure you hire people who understand the forest ecosystem.*

His new foreman produced results. He trimmed staff, cut budgets and focused on worker efficiency. The bottom line was always black ink. *The trees were thinned, the brush was cut and everything was in its place. The new foreman imposed "order" on the forest.* Employee satisfaction dropped and over time, the workload placed on them proved to be too much. Tempers flared, quality dropped and a union was created.

The founder couldn't understand what was going on. He had trusted his managers and thought they did a good job! How could things reach such a state? *If a forest is thinned beyond reason, the existing trees cannot prevent the wind or elements from bringing down the larger trees, destroying the smaller ones and destroying the ecosystem.*

The owner eventually turned the business over to his son. His son was different and understood the management of a business and the people who make it happen. *All of the elements of a forest need to be nurtured and tended, not just the trees.* The son made changes where they needed to be made. He replaced some of the managers and involved more of the employees in operations and decision making. He saw the value and wisdom of the front-line employees and wanted to know what they thought. He asked them how the company could be more productive. He shared his vision of where they were going, set expectations, and then provided the proper training and tools to meet those expectations. *The renewed forest has all the different plants and trees firmly rooted. The soil is held firm and new life is created. It might look like chaos, but the entire ecosystem is sharing the load, resulting in sustained growth.*

Today, ABC Millwork is a national organization, employs hundreds of people, has a reputation for quality and is managed with a sense of vision. It is an elegant example of how a different, more nurturing, perspective can turn a company around.

We must learn to think differently than we have in the past.

In his book, *The Best Of Business Anecdotes*, Peter Hay tells a wonderful story. I retell it here: Herbert Hoover, the president everyone was blaming for the Depression, was not popular during the early 1930's. One day, he was walking down a street in Washington, D.C., with his equally unpopular Secretary of The Treasury, Andrew Mellon. Hoover realized that he had left the White House without any money. He turned to Mellon and said, "Andy, lend me a nickel. I have to call a friend."

Mellon dug in his pocket and gave Hoover a coin, saying, "Here's a dime. You can call both of them."

Hoover's administration of the country and the Depression years is a study in organizational design and application. The country faced tough challenges. Hoover, with the best of intentions, tried to move the country out of the Depression with thinking developed prior to the Depression. It didn't work. Franklin Delano Roosevelt understood that more was needed. He took a cue from Einstein. If you want to get different results, you have to change the thinking and the "system" that produced the previous results. Roosevelt considered the fundamental needs of the American people. He told them what he planned to do to meet those needs and he addressed their spirit.

What is needed now in our corporate culture is similar to what Roosevelt gave the country in the thirties. We need a new approach, a new attitude, a new definition of who we are. And, as happened in the thirties, the change must come from the top.

If the change is to be successful, it must be communicated to everyone in a way that applies to them and, as happened with Roosevelt, renews their spirits, in this case for their work. It boils down to integrity, justice, and leaders who recognize the spiritual side in all of us. I'm not suggesting that we throw away the sound principles of doing business. I'm not suggesting that the leadership become so sensitive and "nice" that they forget to make a profit. What I am suggesting is that success is not just a number on the bottom line of the current income statement. It is also what is being built for the future and what it costs in human terms for those numbers to appear.

We can choose to be profitable companies that nourish and inspire our workers. Or, we can be organizations that squeeze that extra little bit and increase today's bottom line by taking just a little too much out of the people who work for us. We can view the employer/employee relationship as one that is mutually beneficial financially and humanly, or we can continue to view the other guy as someone to "get a little more from."

And it does work both ways. The employees can't point their fingers at management if they are smuggling home office supplies, playing computer games on company time, and calling in sick to play golf. The inhabitants of corporate America, employer and employee, must ask a new question. Instead of, "Am I getting everything out of this I can?" they need to ask, "Am I fulfilling my side of the contract?"

When we make this shift, and we can make it, we won't believe what happens to the productivity in this country. It will go through the roof, and the ripple effects throughout our society will be profound.

We must be careful, however, not to make a change just for the sake of change. Different is not always better. There are many examples of companies that invested heavily in new ideas with little, or even disastrous result. Everyone has worked for, or knows someone who works for, a corporation that rolls out a new organizational chart with alarming regularity. Clearly the last chart didn't fix the perceived problems, nor the one before that. So why do they still try to fix things with a new chart? I would suggest that at the root of many of these companies' malfunctions is not an organizational problem. In fact, it's not a problem of logic at all. It is merely a loss of faith.

When I refer to a loss of faith, I don't refer directly to the faith one might find in the Bible or the Torah, although those definitions of faith will prevail long after OSHA and EEOC and the labels "downsizing" and "correctness" have disappeared. Instead, I refer to faith as the faith an employer has in the employees and the faith the employees return.

What happens when employees and employers lose faith? Instead of looking for the cause of the loss, both sides often go on the attack. "Management tightens the screws because they're jerks." "The employees are ripping us off; we've got to tighten the screws." Management implements a new policy. This generates a more rigid reaction from the employees and the cycle continues. Each party escalates the misunderstanding. The employees start slacking off because they're angry at management and management is angry at the employees because they're "lazy."

In his book, *The Economics of Trust: Liberating Profits and Restoring Corporate Vitality,* prominent turnaround expert, author, and professor at Columbia University, John Whitney, addresses this issue. Whitney states that mistrust (which I refer to as a loss of faith) in an organization doubles direct costs, pulls attention from customers, stifles innovation and drains organization and individual energy. Mistrust can be caused by incompetence, misalignment of performance measures with the reward system, untrustworthy information or a lack of management integrity.

In the corporate world, loss of faith is typically described as disloyalty. Alarmingly, because corporate loyalty is marked as a virtue on the organizational tally sheet, disloyalty is frowned upon. Thus, when an employee experiences enough disappointment in the company to lose faith, our current worldview tells us that employee has lost value to the company. This seems so obviously backward! The employee who has lost faith holds a wealth of information for the manager who is savvy enough to mine it.

I believe it is a rare employee who chooses to become disloyal, and in fact, I even question the label of disloyalty. The great religions of the world don't teach that the opposite of faith is disloyalty. They teach that the opposite of faith is fear. When employees have lost faith in the organization for which they work, they are bound by fear. Their future is uncertain, even if their job is secure. They don't trust that they can continue to enjoy the work which takes up such a large part of their life. And often that fear, justifiably, looks like anger.

How many human resource departments teach employees how to deal with fear? How many managers recognize and respond appropriately to the fear their employees exhibit? How many accountants quantify the costs of inattention to detail or failed quotas in terms of employee loss of faith?

Even the best companies can fall on hard times. When these companies suffer, what they see in their employees is usually not a questioning of the company spirit, it is usually the manifestation of fear of the unknown. The smart leaders see that and can address it honestly within their organizations, freeing the organization to address the direct problems at hand. It harkens back to Roosevelt's "We have nothing to fear, but fear itself."

Let's look at how one leader faced real fear in his organization. In 1998, the finishing plant for The Custom Shoppe, a quality furniture maker in Ixonia, Wisconsin, burned to the ground. The fire spread so quickly that the employees had to run for their lives. Their workplace gone, they were filled with fear for their future. Within twenty-four hours, however, the owner of the company, Frank Krejci, had called a meeting in a local restaurant. "Nobody is going to lose a day of wages on this," he told them. "We're going to continue. But to do that, we have to keep building furniture. We have customers who are expecting their orders to be filled, and we're going to fill them."

Almost immediately, the finishing plant employees were sharing space with another furniture maker, Schweiger Industries, in a small town nearby. In an amazing demonstration of cooperation, the employees of the two companies worked side-by-side to fill orders for their respective customers and pitched in to help one another when needed. The Custom Shoppe shipped two pieces of furniture 96 hours after the fire and had a full truckload two weeks later. Frank did whatever he could to ease the transition and to reassure his workforce. Nobody left the company.

A little over a year later, The Custom Shoppe opened a new facility in Watertown, Wisconsin. At the celebration party, Frank gave each of his employees a pair of sunglasses. "Our future is so bright," he said, "we have to wear shades."

Frank recognized and acknowledged his employees' fears, and then lead them through the difficulties. Like Roosevelt, he came up with a plan and effectively communicated it. He demonstrated his commitment to the people who worked for him in what had to be an extremely difficult circumstance. It might have been easier for him to cut his losses and fold, but he was committed to the well-being of the people who worked for him. They needed their jobs.

Frank Krejci acted with integrity and showed "good faith" at a time when it would be easy for all concerned to lose faith. The employees responded by investing spiritually in their work. They knew they were making a difference and they committed themselves to success. The disillusionment and victimization that could so easily have become the predominant emotion never took hold. The company remained fluid and effective and thrived because of the trust and loyalty the employees placed in their leadership.

Frank Krejci would give all the credit to his employees. In his view, he was blessed with an exceptional workforce. And they were exceptional, because they were given an environment where they were encouraged and allowed to be so.

It is important to point out, however, that Frank Krejci didn't succeed in this simply because it was his goal to do so. He didn't set a goal of "I want to get back in business," and let it go at that. He set into motion a specific, well-defined plan of action. Each step of the plan related to a specific desired outcome that moved him closer to the end goal. The employees were kept informed and were involved in the process from the day of the crisis until the new facility opened. They knew the logic behind the production goals and saw the purpose in them. Everyone worked toward the same end and all could feel the pride of success when the company thrived against all odds.

The case of The Custom Shoppe might be extreme, but it is an obvious example of leadership clearly communicating a specific plan and the reasoning behind the plan.

So often I see management create arbitrary objectives for front-line workers that seem to serve no other function than to put some objectives in place. It is as if the numbers are an end in themselves. The front-line workers are the first to see the lack of integrity in these objectives and the result is a loss of faith. If the leadership wants the company to succeed, it must first know *exactly* what it wants to accomplish. "We want to make a profit," won't do it. That's like saying, "I want to be in the restaurant business," when you really want to be a chef. If you don't know precisely what you want, you're likely to end up with something you didn't expect.

Apart from setting a clear precise course, there is another, equally important step. Leadership must communicate the plan to the employees who are going to carry it out. This is top-down communication so that when the objectives reach the front line, they can be embraced as sound business, an effort people can get behind because the leadership is guiding the ship on a straight and true course.

Just as children need a sense of certainty in their lives to truly thrive, employees need a sense of certainty also to thrive within an organization. There is nothing wrong with a company communicating that it is a safe and secure place in which an employee can invest emotionally. In fact, it is not only okay, but desirable, that employees know that the work they do in the organization can help them grow spiritually as well as professionally. Yet, the behavior of many organizations in this country communicates just the opposite. How, specifically, does this occur?

When a company eliminates senior people to replace them with younger cheaper labor, it communicates to all of the employees that the company cannot be trusted. When the organization adopts and enforces rigid rules that dehumanize the workers and negate the value of their personal lives and obligations, the message is sent out that the company doesn't care about the employees. When the company fails to communicate the forces behind abrupt changes of course, it sends the message to the employees that the leadership is driving blind and that there is no certainty in a secure future. When leadership tolerates dehumanizing management styles, it communicates to the front-line work-ers that they are replaceable and unimportant. They are not safe, they don't belong, they need not invest in the job.

When viewed in this light, these errors of leadership are re-markably easy to see. They embody the old way of viewing the forest. But changes in viewpoint don't always happen overnight. We are restricted by generations of habit and out-of-date think-ing. To know that we must change is not enough, we need to have a plan. We need to get specific.

I challenge leadership to ask these questions:

What is at the heart and soul of our organization? Just saying "people" or talking about company spirit won't get you off the hook. Instead of looking at spirit, try looking at the spiritual. This can be unsettling, and if you're finding yourself resistant to this view, your resistance itself might be a strong indication that you need to try it. What's the worst that can happen? Is it that you might find that your organization is spiritually bankrupt, that all faith is lost, that there is no bonding agent at work at all? That might, indeed, be what you discover, but I contend that is not the worst that can happen. The worst that can happen is for the or-ganization to be spiritually bereft and for the leadership not to realize it.

It is incumbent on leadership to regularly and with inten-tion review every policy and management system in light of the spiritual element. What are the attitudes toward personal time off? How does the company help employees grow in the job? At what personal cost do the employees fulfill their end of the contract and is the price too high? Does the organization communicate to the front-line employees as vital intelligent co-creators of company success?

How do I interact with the people I manage? Am I authoritarian, do I use knowledge as power over them? Evaluate yourself in terms of the negative management styles described in the next chapter and devise a strategy for changing those behaviors you find. You might have to start small. For example, you might make it a weekly goal to solicit input on something, even a small issue, so that you can become accustomed to the action and to accepting responses.

Make no mistake. Leaders must still lead. Employees will still need managers, but give yourself the chance to explore new methods. I once asked a supervisor how she interacted with the people she managed. Her response was immediate. "I involve everyone in everything." This might not be a style that works for everyone, but watching her in action was a joy. Information flowed in her department. The employees were confident and invested. They took pride in their work and productivity was high. There was no doubt that she was the manager of the department, but in her case, the word "leader" described her function perfectly. She was a guide, she set the tone, and she established the structure. Her employees were inspired to give their best effort and if they weren't, she found out why.

This is a frightening model for some people. For many, it is stepping into the void. I think it is much like the way the leadership of our nation must have felt as they commenced the New Deal.

How do I inspire my employees to greatness? This is an interesting concept. Many managers will respond, "I don't need my employees to be great. I just want them to do their job." My answer to that is, you'll be lucky if you can get that much. Taking responsibility for inspiring a workforce is serious work. It requires us to look at ourselves. Do we know how to be inspired? Do we know what lies at the foundation of our inspiration? Do we even aspire to greatness ourselves or are we somehow trying to draw our sense of worth from the employees we oversee? This question drives us to the deeper levels of our own leadership potential in a manner that business schools would say falls into the Religious Studies arena.

I contend that unless managers understand what is at the heart of their own life views as well as they understand management techniques and performance evaluations, they will fail as leaders. They can be bosses, but can they be leaders? Leaders know the answer to "Who Am I?" They have reached a spiritual place where they understand their own humanity and the humanity of those they lead. Leadership is a calling. It is a call to authenticity. It is understanding how to do the right thing for the people they lead. Their motivations are about giving and growing instead of somehow drawing self-worth from a title or from a degree of power over other lives. Leaders inspire greatness, and see the fruit of it in their workplace, by aspiring to greatness themselves and actively encouraging it in others. Anyone who wishes to find true success in an organization must find out if he or she has the courage to dig this deep to become a leader.

What do I do to assist my employees in meeting their goals? Frontline employees must look to leaders for the larger picture. It is the leaders who must ensure that employees have the tools and training to succeed in the tasks set before them. It is the leaders who must offer support and encouragement when difficulties arise. It is the leaders who must help eliminate the barriers between the project at hand and the ultimate success of the project. To put it in athletic terms, the leaders need to go to bat or throw the blocks as well as calling the plays.

So frequently, managers are willing to throw money and materials at a project without investing in it enough themselves to know if what they've done has a chance of succeeding. It is a management copout, used all too frequently, to throw technology at a poorly functioning group and then hold them accountable when the project fails. "I gave you the finest tools. I did my part. What's wrong with you?" I ask, what's wrong with the manager?

What is preventing my employees from investing emotionally in their jobs? This could be another courageous question. What if the answer is, "My attitude?" Or, what if the answer requires bold steps on a manager's part that could cause a loss of collateral with his or her boss? I see the first answer as an opportunity for growth. Finding that a problem is within ourselves at least puts the problem in a place where we can have some control over the outcome, painful as the process might be. The manager who finds the barriers in the attitudes and policies of upper management is in a terrible bind. For a company to truly succeed, leadership starts at the top. It can be extremely difficult to work upstream, and sometimes there is simply no sense in dashing oneself against a concrete dam blocking the way.

And so, even the external barriers can cause soul-searching. In this case, the only advice I can extend is to remember the Berlin Wall. Many individuals died over the decades trying to get across, or under, that wall. But their faith in the belief system was so strong that, one person at a time, the communal belief system changed. The momentum of the belief system became so overwhelming that one day, the wall simply fell. The individual manager who is stuck between a wall of upper management and a poor situation has to decide whether to risk jumping over the wall, living with the wall and holding onto his or her values, or sneaking out of the country.

Do I know what I love to do? Do I know what my employees love to do? It is so easy to draw boxes on a chart and plunk names into them. We tend to write job descriptions and then force people into the description. Do we, as managers and leaders, recognize our own strengths and weaknesses and those of our employees so that we can reorganize the task load to utilize the strengths of each individual? People who enjoy what they are doing do it well. Why create cookie-cutter jobs when a little negotiation gets the job done better? Let's say you have two accounts receivable clerks. Each of them is responsible for checking and coding invoices, entering them in the computer, and making low-key collection calls. One person is bored by the number crunching and the other hates making the phone calls. While it would ruin the symmetry of the organizational job description, would it be so bad to give the one clerk more paperwork and assign the other all of the collection calls? There is little doubt that more work would be processed, there would be fewer errors, and collections would probably go up. And all that is required to elicit this effect is for a manager to take the time to ask these clerks, "What do you enjoy doing? Is there a better way to do what you're doing? Do you need anything from me to help you do your job better?"

This isn't rocket science, but in many organizations it is a radical idea because they are stuck in the old forest viewpoint of tidying up the undergrowth and trying to make all the trees look the same.

A thriving organization requires a diversity of talent. A stand of groomed tall trees might satisfy our human need for order, but in many ways the "chaotic order" of a mature forest is more fruit-ful and more sustainable. Instead of exerting energy to make our organizations fit the boxes, it is time to look at, and respect, the unique contributions each employee can make. We can no longer afford to rely on the old style of autocratic management. We are focusing our efforts in the wrong place.

Whether consciously or not, all members of the workplace seek some sort of spiritual nourishment from their work life. They need to know the value of their work and they need to believe in their mission. They would not be human if this were not true. Employees know this, but our management traditions ignore it. Since the Industrial Revolution, employees have been regarded as part of the machinery. It is dehumanizing, and in a world where creativity is becoming increasingly valued, it is counterproduc-tive. We can no longer take any aspect of our corporate spiritual message for granted. It is evidenced in the way we view our em-ployees and our customers. We cannot afford to assume that our employees know what is expected of them and why, nor can we assume that a paycheck buys employee investment.

American business has what it takes to create and imple-ment a new view, and the time for it is now. The leadership, the tall trees, of corporate America must lead the way and keep the new vision in view so that all participants in the workplace, even those who work in the shade of others, can contribute in a full and satisfying way.

WE CONTINUE TO SEE MANAGEMENT AND LEADERSHIP

ASSIGNMENTS AS A REWARD AND A RIGHT.

LEADERSHIP IS A CALLING, ONE THAT REQUIRES AN

ETHICAL RELATIONSHIP TO PEOPLE AND

A DEEP COMMITMENT TO PRODUCTIVITY

AND THE COMMON GOOD.

MANAGEMENT BEHAVIORS THAT DESTROY PRODUCTIVITY

"Let us lie in wait for the righteous man, because he is inconvenient to us and opposes our actions; he reproaches us of sins against the law, and accuses us for sins against our training."

Wisdom of Solomon
Chapter 2:3

We have many terrific managers and leaders in America. My hat goes off to them. There are others, however, who out of ignorance or personal weakness create the majority of the problems in America's organizations. I think most of us simply try to avoid confrontation with these people. We work around them, we adapt, we shrug our shoulders and ask, "What can we do?" without ever expecting an answer.

Partly, we are uncertain about how to proceed, because on the surface, these managers are working from established, and often perceived as positive, aspects of the workplace. The distinction is that these people have gone to the extreme and have manifested a behavior out of personal weakness instead of from a sound management perspective. It's a potentially good thing gone bad. The trick is to see when they've crossed the line.

Over the years I have worked with many companies and organizations and have come to identify eighteen destructive management behaviors. You might know more. I've seen them in all kinds of settings from manufacturing to government, and I've seen them manifested with varying degrees of intensity. I've found that once you identify somebody's behavior, and there might be more than one, you can almost predict his or her next move. I've also come to fully appreciate the damage these people do to a corporate culture and to the workers they employ.

I've always believed that identifying a problem is the first step to solving it. And, therefore, I offer you the following categories of harmful management styles. If you recognize them in members of your own management team, it's important to understand one thing: someone is letting them stay in your organization. Whether by neglect or with intent, your company "system" is supporting their behavior. And, it is costing the company money. Lots of it.

By the time you've read this book, I hope you will have a clear picture on just how expensive it is, in human terms and in dollars and cents, to allow a destructive environment to exist in the workplace. But for now, let's look at some of the symptoms and some ways we can respond to them.

A word of caution: These descriptions are my generalizations in an attempt to communicate a concept. Please do not use them as the basis for a corporate cleansing. That is not my intent. Unless you have looked deeply at a situation, it would be easy to recognize some element of behavior I describe on the following pages and immediately and unfairly attach a label to someone who doesn't deserve it. Sometimes the symptoms of a disease are present where there may be no disease at all. I would suggest that even the best leaders have exhibited some of these traits from time to time.

Also, I recognize that sometimes we are forced to reconcile ourselves to the continuing presence of a key person. There are circumstances where without one individual, things would disintegrate. Just be certain that this dependence is the reality of the situation instead of the perception.

I also need to mention that I have speculated about the psychological or emotional motivations of some people. I do so in the spirit of freedom of speech. I am not a psychologist. I merely offer my own take on the situation in general. If it helps my readers to look more closely at some of the destructive systems in the American workplace, or if the leadership begins to watch for problems they've ignored in the past, I have achieved my goal in outlining these behaviors. I offer a subjective perspective, not a therapeutic diagnosis.

I've offered some professional strategies for dealing with each behavior. Again, these are my generalizations, not strict recipes. The best strategies for you will depend on the environment you work in, the kind of work you do, your personality, and your role in the organization. I've mixed in examples from both the blue collar and the white collar world, but the behaviors are not limited to either environment.

I have assigned each of the behaviors an acronym. You don't need to memorize them, but you'll see them in the text as I address each style. Also, it isn't necessary to read all eighteen styles sequentially. Feel free to read a few and then jump forward to the other chapters, returning to these later. I encourage you to read them all at some point, however. I include several management styles we don't typically view as destructive. You won't want to miss any.

I'm guessing that as you scan the list that follows, you'll already be nodding your head in recognition. And, if you suspect you might see yourself in any of these, take heart. Have the courage to keep reading. Be angry at me, disagree with me, but at least let me have my say and take a look at the workplace from my perspective.

THE EIGHTEEN DESTRUCTIVE MANAGEMENT STYLES

BIOPM	Blame It On Performance Measures
BOT	Big On Titles
DDBTM	Don't Do it Better Than Me
DRB	Don't Rock the Boat
IDHAC	I Don't Have A Clue
IDYL	I Demand Your Loyalty
INQB	I Never Question the Boss
ITAC	I Take All the Credit
JPBH	Just Plain Butt Head
MBFOM	Management By Flavor Of the Month
MBLOL	Management By Length Of the Leash
MDOF	My Door is Open to Favorites
MNOE	My Name is On Everything
MODC	Master Of Damage Control
SFVA	Searching For Value-Added
STATTS	Stand There And Take it To Survive
TMIB	Trust Me, I'm the Boss
WIIFM	What's In It For Me?

BIOPM
BLAME IT ON PERFORMANCE MEASURES

"The greatest disservice the Harvard Business School has ever played on corporate America is management by objectives."

James Mcmanus, Chairman
Marketing Corporation of America

BIOPMs are numbers people. They believe in numbers, they generate numbers, and they rule by numbers. And, in many cases, they were told in school that their numbers will somehow motivate their employees. I view performance objectives and measures as an attempt to make management a science instead of a skill. They enable people who don't want to interact with the human aspect of workers the opportunity to hold jobs that are labeled management, but are really something else. Please understand that I am not railing against goal-setting. I am objecting to the damage that occurs when the goal-setting becomes the result instead of a marker toward achieving a result.

I have seen case after case where productive, valuable employees were down-sized because their numbers on some arbitrary performance measure weren't as high as somebody else's. Unfortunately, the numbers don't take into account dependability, loyalty, leadership, flexibility, or a host of other important workplace attributes. So often the decisions based on numbers are bad ones, and it seems that everyone knows it but management.

My beef with BIOPM managers, however, isn't just that they rule by numbers which might not have any bearing on the real issues behind productivity or customer satisfaction. They also hide behind them. It's difficult to hold numbers accountable, and therefore, the rationale goes, generate more numbers and you're safe. Numbers are clean, they don't cry in your office, they don't need time off, and they don't disagree with the person who created them. And, because they are embraced by the current management mythology, a facility in creating performance objectives and other statistics to support them is a real plus in the climb up the corporate ladder.

Most BIOPMs are masters at ladder climbing. If you're very good at numbers, you can use them to make yourself look good no matter what. You can use them as political weapons against other managers who also want to move up, and you can use them to justify almost any decision you make.

There is a cynicism that develops amongst people who work with a BIOPM. It is fairly certain that once a performance objective has been met, a new performance measure will automatically replace it. For most workers, a performance measure is like working with a dysfunctional track coach who is focused on the high jump. You don't necessarily get any training for the high jump, and you can't raise or lower the bar based on your ability. The bar is the same for everyone. And, regardless of your strengths at the discus or as a sprinter, your value as part of the track and field team is evaluated on how high you jump, because that is what the coach is measuring.

Professional Strategy:

If you are inclined to be a numbers person:

- Be sure your numbers, goals, and expectations are customer driven. This will ensure the integrity of your numbers.
- Remember to look at the whole person and the intangibles, not just the numbers in appraisals.
- Check your numbers for validity. Beware of arbitrary numbers if they are going to affect your workers in a negative way.
- Communicate your thinking behind the numbers to the people who will be held accountable for meeting your objectives.
- Listen to the employees. They might already have the equation worked out in a way you never would have considered.
- Be certain that your objectives complement the objectives of the organization.
- Consider the costs of meeting the objectives in real and in human terms.
- Resist the impulse to solve problems by assigning new objectives.

If you are an employee:

- Be sure *your* numbers are right if you ever challenge him or her.

If you manage a BIOPM:

- Be sure the BIOPM has had training in system process tools to ensure that he or she at least knows how to use numbers properly.

- Keep an eye on employee morale. Be sure the performance measures are necessary and that they aren't moving targets.

- Invest in management training for this individual that focuses on other methods of motivation and evaluation.

BOT

BIG ON TITLES

"I awoke one morning and found myself famous."

George Gordon Byron
English poet and satirist

I have to think that BOTs believe that a promotion auto-matically reorganizes a DNA string in their bodies that makes them worthy, finally, of respect and recognition. The acquisition of a title has somehow changed them relative to the rest of the world in a way they were unable to establish previously, and their satisfaction in their new title, not their new job, is boundless. At least for awhile. BOTs are looking for external validation and can never get enough.

For BOTs it is important to have their titles emblazoned on everything: their stationery, door, parking space, holiday greeting cards and even on their thank you notes. It's easy for us to brush off this obsession with titles as harmless and even humorous. We might smile as we notice that before making a statement in a meeting, BOTs introduce themselves with special emphasis on their title, or at least mention their title during the discussion. And of course, this would be appropriate in a setting where everyone doesn't know one another, but a BOT is often so compulsive about his or her title that it's mentioned even in a roomful of people who are well acquainted.

I contend that this is a danger signal we need to learn to watch. Don't get me wrong. Titles are important, and in business transactions they are often imperative. The issue is about the degree of focus. Can a BOT have a human-to-human interaction in the workplace without the title being part of the equation? I doubt it.

Let me give you an example. I once worked with a man who was a BOT. We both held the same title for quite some time until he was given a promotion. About a year later, we were in a meeting together, and without thinking anything of it, I referred to him by his name. After the meeting, he called me on the telephone and said, "Art, we are friends, but when we are in a meeting, I want you to refer to me by my title first, then by my name." I was floored, but I'd learned an important lesson.

BOTs are always looking for what is viewed as important to others and then they must have it. In my coworker's case, he required a respectful distance at least, or maybe even reverence. Other BOTs might require that their name and title be on important projects, even if they aren't personally doing the work. Another characteristic, and this one is especially dangerous, is that the BOT needs to be The Decision Maker.

I was once giving a training session and asked the students how they viewed a particular problem in their organization and what they saw as potential solutions. This group was so well-conditioned that it took some prodding to get them past, "That's a management decision that only the director makes." This wasn't a director-only decision in my view. I felt the class was well qualified to work on the problem, but their Director apparently took his Title seriously. He directed their work, he directed their environment, and he came close to directing their thoughts.

A BOT who needs deference and authority will have tremendous energy for drawing lines around employees and productivity, because if the lines aren't drawn carefully, then the areas within the lines can't be "managed" and there won't be much use for the "manager." If the organization is functioning well without the titled person dispensing decisions large and small, the title loses its punch. The BOT becomes just another player on the team and to the BOT, that would be devastating.

The BOT is an excellent example of potentially desirable behaviors gone bad. Of course we want leaders who aren't afraid to make a decision. Of course we want a degree of ambition for advancement in our workforce. The problem is that for the BOT, a pending decision supports the title, instead of the title supporting the decision. The motivation is backward. For BOTs, the golden ring is always brighter on somebody else's merry-go-round and as soon as the luster of the present title wears off, they look for the next one, the one that will really mean that they are worthwhile people.

We can feel sorry for these people and even empathize with them to a degree, but can we afford to have them in positions of responsibility in our organizations? Their problems won't go away, and the farther they advance—and they can go a long way because they can master the right look and the right talk—the more damage they can do in terms of demoralizing and undermining the workplace.

Let me give you one more example to serve as a contrast.

I had the opportunity to work with a company in the Midwest, providing some management training. I met with a management team before the training to set the content and focus for the first session, which would be from 4:00 to 8:00 PM, and would include a working dinner. Dress was casual.

When I entered the room, a few management personnel came up and introduced themselves by name, no titles, and the session began. In cases like this, the CEO usually comes up and makes a few comments then goes home. I was surprised when no CEO was introduced and the manager who got things rolling brought me up immediately. I figured the CEO must be late or was going to be a no show.

At the break, I asked one of the employees about the CEO and she motioned to a man who had introduced himself to me before the session began. "That's Frank over there," she said. "He attends all management training." What a contrast between this man, who was not only at the training, but walking around the room chatting with the employees, and the typical CEO types who "don't have time" to go to management training themselves!

It was fascinating to watch the dynamic in this company. Not only did everyone approach Frank and one another with ease, it appeared that they all took turns talking and listening. The atmosphere was relaxed, but enthusiastic. There were no BOTs in that room and therefore titles didn't get in the way of the company self-organizing to be efficient, creative, and productive. In this company, the only title that mattered was "customer." Their CEO, Frank, was leader, visionary, student, and mentor. He was doing what he knew best—being Frank—and he set the tone for the rest to follow.

Professional Strategy:

If you suspect you're a member of the BOT Brigade:

- First, relax. You might never have viewed your obsession with titles in the terms I described above. You might have bought into a corporate norm that you now want to question.

- Second, take a look at your motivation. If you suspect you're Big On Titles because of the external validation, it couldn't hurt to work on why. Your quest for external validation will only get in your way as you go through life. If you've gotten far enough to have earned a title, you clearly have something going for you. Time to find out for yourself.

If you work for, or with, someone who is Big On Titles:

- It's not a good situation, because the BOT can cause mischief in terms of control problems and employee morale. But, as far as getting along with a BOT, that's fairly easy to do. Honor the title, at least as much as you can. Or, to put it bluntly, give the BOT lots of strokes.

- Don't get into situations with them where they see you as competition. BOTs will usually engage in, or create, power struggles if threatened, and the results can be messy.

- If your BOT is way off the deep end, requiring excessive deference, dig into the policy manual. If the BOT is outside of the company policy, you might be able to get some relief. Otherwise, maybe you need to ask that a policy be established.

DDBTM
DON'T DO IT BETTER THAN ME

*"If you think your boss is stupid, remember: You wouldn't have a job
if he was any smarter."*

Albert A. Grant
American Society of Civil Engineers

Jealousy in the workplace, as in private life, can be one of
the most destructive forces in relationships. Unfortunately, in the
workplace, when the jealousy is felt by a person in power, the
destruction is usually visited upon the innocent. To me, the
DDBTM is like a soldier in a foxhole ready to shoot down anything that looks like something noteworthy they didn't think of
or do themselves. They are insecure and afraid of anything that
shines the spotlight on anyone other than themselves.

Working for a DDBTM means constant frustration for employees who have anything on the ball. Either their creativity is
stifled or they find themselves being singled out for unwarranted
punishments. Top-notch employees working for a DDBTM will
find their manager looking for any excuse to get on their case.
Ten minutes late coming back for lunch, a personal phone call on
company time even though everyone logged overtime the day
before, or any small work imperfection are all fair game for a "talking to." If a creative employee comes up with an especially creative idea, "it just can't be done."

Employees who want to punch the clock and go home will probably do fine with this management style, but employees who have the potential to really contribute to the company will quickly become unmotivated and will probably be lost to the company either through attrition or the development of a poor attitude. This would be bad enough if the damage stopped there, but as with most destructive management styles, this one thrives on behind-the-scenes, or shall we say behind-the-back tactics.

One of the hallmarks of a DDBTM manager is that he or she will downplay or criticize an idea or project to the people who presented it, but will quickly turn around and present the idea as his or her own to upper management. This kind of betrayal can't do anything good for an organization, and unfortunately, as a company begins to see the problems the DDBTM causes, they become so preoccupied with trying to address the symptoms that they never recognize the source of the problems.

Working with a DDBTM from a management perspective is also difficult. DDBTMs have to start somewhere. After all, they are probably the kids who in first grade constantly jumped up and down in class saying, "Teacher, look at what I did!" If you have an employee who is a DDBTM, you have to be vigilant. The hard feelings and divisiveness such an individual can create will quickly undo any team building you might have attempted.

If you have a DDBTM in the management ranks with you, watch out! If you are worth your salt, this person will slice and dice you at every opportunity. The ideal situation is if he or she can humiliate you in front of a group, but there are no rules against going behind your back, either. In fact, if the person is really keyed in on you as a competitor, you'll probably get smiles to your face and stabs in the back. They might even present themselves as allies to your cause so they can get the inside track and have more leverage to use against you later.

The problem with a DDBTMs is that they are hard to nail down. After all, there is nothing wrong with having an honest difference of opinion. Nor is there anything wrong with having a change of heart after some consideration. This happens to every-one. The only difference is that for most of us it is nothing more than a disagreement or change of heart. With the DDBTM these are handy excuses to hide behind while waging guerrilla warfare against anyone he or she perceives as superior in any way.

I was once making a proposal to a screening committee for a community program I had been hired to put together. During the presentation meeting, one individual continually, and aggressively, shot holes in my ideas. My proposal was deemed to be of little merit and I was out the door. Soon after, I learned that my pro-posal, with some slight modification, had been presented to the larger body by this same individual, who of course took all of the credit for it.

Another time I was working with an organization and watched a DDBTM in action. This supervisor happened to have a very capable and project-oriented assistant who had put together a proposal for a conference presentation. Before the presentation was ready, it was agreed that the assistant would go to the conference and present the work. When the assistant went over the presentation with the DDBTM, however, the DDBTM criticized it sharply, questioned its purpose, and told the assistant that she would not be going to the conference after all. The DDBTM would have to do it. Of course the presentation was given almost unchanged and the DDBTM took all the credit.

While these behaviors look like the I Take All the Credit management style you'll see later, there is one big difference. The DDBTM must devastate his or her victims before taking their goods and running off with them. What is so startling about these people is that their search and destroy tactics are often so subtle that only those they've injured can recognize them.

To most of the organization, the DDBTM takes a low profile. They want it known that they are the top of the heap, but they don't want to have to continually prove it by doing anything flashy or profound. Instead, they quietly lie in wait and strike when the damage to others is greatest, and therefore in their eyes, the benefit to them is optimal. When something they are not involved in begins to look too good, and it's clear they won't be able to steal it for their own glory, suddenly the policies and procedures manuals come out and the project begins to look a bit shaky. They seek "clarification" and then run to the boss with enough "concerns" to kill anything that moves.

Professional Strategy:

If you think you might be a DDBTM:

- Well, frankly, I don't believe anyone *will* think he or she is a DDBTM. I think the internal defenses and rationalization systems have to be so strong in these individuals that they certainly won't have read this far, or will only read it to see who they can accuse of being one. If you are truly concerned that you might be a DDBTM, ask your employees and ask your co-managers for feedback. (But don't ask any DDBTMs, they will tell you that you are, even if you aren't!)

If you work for, or with, someone who is a DDBTM:

- Don't trust him or her with any information that might be used against you, no matter how friendly and empathetic the DDBTM might appear on a given day.

If you are an employee:

- Try to let unfounded, hurtful comments roll off your back. It's probably not about you.
- Be careful not to overshadow him or her.
- Consider moving to a different department where

your talents will be appreciated and rewarded.

If you manage a DDBTM:

- Formalize recognition within the area. Require the DDBTM to formally and publicly give pats on the back on a scheduled basis.

- Encourage delegation. Ask the DDBTM to give you a review of the strengths of people in his or her department and help the DDBTM plan opportunities for the employees to shine.

- Be sure to compliment the DDBTM when praise is appropriate. If he or she is getting praise for his or her own efforts, maybe stealing someone else's thunder will be less important.

- Provide positive reinforcement when the DDBTM gives recognition to others.

DRB

DON'T ROCK THE BOAT

"Things do not change; we change."

Henry David Thoreau
Walden

Have you ever been in a rowboat with someone who is afraid of water? Remember rocking the boat a little bit? What happened? Your passenger probably started to become uncomfortable, then moved to paranoia and maybe got angry at you. It's not really the water that frightens them, it's what will happen if they end up in it that scares them.

The same is true of the DRB management style. They are quite content to be in the corporate boat as long as it doesn't tip or start taking on water. They do everything they can to maintain a quiet status quo while they are at the helm. Anything that makes waves or muddies the waters makes them uncomfortable, and if someone comes along to really shake things up, they panic.

While on the surface, the peaceful scenario sounds fine, and maybe even desirable, let's take a careful look at what it costs to maintain those quiet waters.

The imaginations of DRBs are about 8 1/2x11 inches. This is the size of the office memo. They thrive on setting up an *In* box, processing the paperwork and then routing it through the *Out* box. While not all DRBs do this, some appear highly organized or even obsessive about filing systems and order. They love memos, and one suspects that if they could sit quietly at their desks all day and handle everything via paperwork, they'd be happy. To the DRB, paper in motion is a sign of productivity. If someone approaches them with a great idea, they might respond, "Write it up and I'll take a look at it." They don't like to make decisions on the spot and if something is likely to shake up the current system, their impulse is to let the idea die a slow death. If a decision is unavoidable, a group decision or running the idea by the next management level is much preferred over deciding alone.

DRBs also don't deal well with Type A personalities. They often don't like change at all, and they certainly don't want things to move too quickly. They will "what if..." projects into the ground. From a dollars and cents point of view, this reluctance to move can be disastrous. From a corporate morale point of view, it's like giving the company a shot of Novocain. The high-energy idea people and the DRBs will be at constant odds and will frustrate one another endlessly. Unfortunately for the DRBs, they often develop a reputation as corporate weenies. Instead of keeping the boat afloat in calm waters, all too often DRB's leave the organization stuck in the mud.

Professional Strategy:

If you think you might be a DRB:

- Make an honest assessment of your strengths and weaknesses. Are you being utilized to the best of your ability, or are you trying to do a job that runs against your nature?

- Recognize that your resistance to change frustrates some people around you. Take responsibility for it and communicate clearly with others about how you process information.

- Be sure you know what you enjoy about your job and what you don't enjoy. The worst thing for a DRB, and for the organization in which he or she works, is to be doing the wrong job for his or her personality. If necessary, go to a career counselor and make sure you're doing what you should be doing.

- DRBs often survive well in intensely bureaucratic environments. This means, they usually don't lose their jobs even if they are dragging things to the bottom of the pool. Don't settle for surviving. Make the change, as much as you hate it. If the organization won't move you out of a bad position for you, move yourself. Take charge of your career and happiness.

If you work for or with a DRB:

- Don't expect the DRB to get excited by your exciting ideas for improving things or by your creative thinking in general.
- When you need something, propose things in small pieces. Give the DRB some time to chew things over. Plan ahead so the project deadline doesn't suffer.
- Recognize what makes them comfortable. A memo might get a better response than a telephone call.
- Don't back a DRB against the wall and demand an immediate decision.
- If you need decisive action taken on an issue, prepare to be frustrated. This is the environment you're in and it probably won't change. Figure out how to make it work for you.

If you are an employee:

- DRBs are masters of procrastination. Find ways to nudge them without being in their face, if possible.

IDHAC

I Don't Have A Clue

"If a blind person leads a blind person, they both will fall in a pit."
Matthew 15:14

I feel bad for the IDHACs. Often they are not to blame for their being in management positions for which they are ill-suited. They didn't know they were ill-suited. Often, the IDHAC is a nice person, a company favorite, who had climbed to the top of his or her pay scale. Once there, the company didn't want to hurt any feelings, and so when the time came, a minor reclassification and *voila*, the problem was solved. The IDHAC was now ready to advance up the pay scale ladder and wreak all kinds of havoc along the way.

IDHACs are a little like Mr. Magoo. While trying to help the little old ladies across the street, they are oblivious to the traffic pileups they're creating. IDHACs have trouble seeing the big picture. Often, they don't even see the little picture. They usually know they're in over their heads and often react to it by retreating into a state of mental gridlock.

Because they aren't able to plan for the long term, they have limited vision and no larger sense of leadership. IDHACs eventually settle into a pattern of daily crisis management. They become masters of short-term thinking. Their gratification comes from quick decisions and immediate results. Brushfires abound.

Some IDHACs might manage this short-term focus reasonably well, but most of their employees see that their manager is flailing in the dark and the result is low morale and alienation from the organization. Sometimes, the IDHAC is simply ignored by the employees. This costs organizations in both real and in human terms. The talents of the employees are wasted and the IDHAC might be implementing short-term solutions that cost long-term money.

Of all the destructive management characteristics, this one might be the most tragic because it is so avoidable. If a company is promoting within, the personnel being considered require investment well down the road, before they get the new sign on the new office door. They need to be mentored and involved in training and evaluation to see whether they have what it takes to lead, and if they like the idea of the new role. If the lines in the organization can be kept fluid, this type of training and evaluation can be almost invisible. The candidates grow into their jobs and the company knows what they are getting before the candidate arrives behind the bigger desk.

We need to stop looking at promotions as a reward for doing the existing job well. There needs to be an opportunity for the individual to grow in the job, but the opportunity must be presented when there is some indication that the promotion will be successful. Clueless managers are like an anchor around the neck of the organization. IDHACs might be nice people, but their inability to function in a management position is a tragedy that is all too common.

Professional Strategy:

If you think you might be an IDHAC:

- Find a mentor. Now.
- Beware of making quick decisions for the sake of making a decision.
- Find ways to get informed. Ask questions. You don't have to know everything already, and if your organization thinks you do, it isn't the right place for you.
- Absorb everything.
- Listen to your employees and solicit input in a professional way. Don't get entrenched in trying to know everything. You'll look ridiculous.
- Attend a well-defined program on personal productivity and project management.

If you work for or with an IDHAC:

- When you need something, give him or her as much information as possible in a clear fashion. Make things a no-brainer whenever possible.
- While decisive decision-making is admirable in a leader, don't encourage an IDHAC to make impulsive decisions. Leaders make quick decisions

based on knowledge and understanding. IDHACs make quick decisions from panic.

If you are an employee:

- You have every right to be frustrated and alienated, even if the IDHAC is a "nice guy." Stop beating yourself up.

If you manage an IDHAC:

- Be a mentor. Involve the IDHAC in every opportunity to learn more about how things work.

- Be hands on. Train the person to do the job. Work through tasks and thought processes together until the IDHAC gains confidence.

IDYL

I DEMAND YOUR LOYALTY

"Yesterday I was a dog. Today I am a dog. Tomorrow I'll probably still be a dog."

Snoopy

The IDYL management style is one of the most recognizable of the destructive management styles. Unfortunately, it is not always recognized as detrimental to an organization, because loyalty is undoubtedly a positive quality in an organization. The problem with IDYLs is that they go too far. Loyalty becomes some kind of ongoing test instead of a form of commitment.

The IDYL style consists of three components: control, conformity, and loyalty. To many upper level managers, these three drives are admirable and they often view the IDYL as someone doing a tough job that someone has to do for the company to succeed.

IDYLs often look good on paper. Their numbers are good. They care about the company. Because loyalty is so important to the IDYLs, their own corporate loyalty permeates their private lives. It wouldn't be too surprising to find the company logo emblazoned on their pajamas! They see themselves as instruments of the company, and because they are often skilled speakers and organizers, they usually get results. What organization wouldn't feel fortunate to have such a manager?

Unfortunately, IDYLs can do much more harm than good. They take what is a potentially positive attribute and take it to the extreme. Upper management typically won't see the downside of this, but the people who work for the IDYL will, and they will be embittered by it. One of the warning signs for this behavior is when a manager identifies so closely with the organization that he or she begins to use terms such as "my building," "my section," "my people" in a way that implies ownership instead of location. Also, the IDYL will overreact to personnel problems and employee complaints. It gets personal. To the IDYL, failure on the part of the employees to exhibit unfailing loyalty to the IDYL is interpreted as disloyalty to the organization itself. It is unacceptable.

The IDYL manager becomes unrealistic and unbending in the demand for loyalty. The employee must conform. There is usually only one appropriate way to respond to a situation and the employee had better guess what that is. People, projects, and performance are balanced on a narrow wire in a conditional and judgmental atmosphere. Ultimately, the IDYL institutes a ritualistic set of controls that forces the employee to honor the manager instead of the company. The employee's measure of personal productivity becomes, on a daily basis, how he stands with the IDYL, not how truly productive he was.

IDYLs smell fear and thrive on it. They believe that fear keeps people in line. It keeps them on the narrow track the IDYL has determined is the right track. Machines can work well in such a rigid world, but it can be hard on humans. If an employee even questions an IDYL, the question itself is interpreted as a personal challenge to their authority. The questioner might be viewed as disloyal and banished to a different level of the pecking order.

I once worked for an IDYL who sat me down in my office and offered to help my career if I would give him my undying loyalty. Those were his exact words. I said "no" and my career in that organization was hell on wheels for several years. This person eventually flamed out in the organization. I was still hanging on and things got better for me, but it was a rough ride over me saying that terrible "N" word, no.

Because IDYLs masquerade as such good people for the company, and it certainly can't be questioned that they believe they have the company's best interests at heart, it is very difficult for other managers to see any problems. If an IDYL works for a Don't Rock The Boat type, you have a combination you'll never break up. The IDYL keeps the waters flat, is loyal to the core, and the DRB doesn't have to ask a lot of questions.

It all sounds kind of okay until you look at the job satisfaction, potential for personal growth, and real productivity of the employees who work for the IDYL. The garden the IDYL tends might get enough water and sunlight to bear a little fruit, but it won't ever thrive and be bountiful.

Professional Strategy:

If you think you might be an IDYL:

- You are probably extremely bright and competent. Know that you can do even more good for your organization if you can figure out ways to optimize the unique qualities of the individuals you employ.

- Find a mentor who is not an IDYL but *whom you respect.* It won't do you any good to pair up with the Don't Rock the Boat person who has a vested interest in keeping you like you are. Find someone who can discuss management philosophy with you in terms of specific individuals and functions. Find someone who will stretch you.

- Relax a little. It takes a lot of energy to funnel everyone into the same shape. Let your employees be who they are a bit more. You'll be healthier for it.

If you work for or with an IDYL:

- Don't buy into the loyalty issue. You can be loyal to the organization and to yourself without conforming to some narrow definition of appropriate behavior and ideology. You can work for an IDYL, cautiously, without losing sight of the company or your governing values.

- Realize that IDYLs believe they are acting in an ethical manner. They believe they are right.

If you are an employee:

- Be careful, and know that you won't be rewarded for thinking or acting outside the box. If you don't expect reward, it's not as troubling when you don't get it!

- The IDYL will compromise employees for the good of the company. Be careful. Try to find a few points on which you can agree with the IDYL and be sure he or she knows where you stand on those issues. It will boost your longevity in the organization and make things easier for you in difficult situations.

If you manage an IDYL:

- Model that you value others' time away from work and that you recognize that different people have different needs and approaches.

- Monitor the situation to be sure the loyalty demands haven't become so extreme and personal that employees feel threatened.

INQB
I Never Question the Boss

"Good followers do not become good leaders."

Laurence J. Peter
University of Southern California

Middle managers who never question their boss are a common, difficult to eradicate weed in the corporate garden. If their employees were in charge, they'd be gone in an instant, but because the INQB bends over backwards to please his or her immediate supervisor and other management levels above that, the bosses are always pleased. Therefore the INQB remains.

Managers with this characteristic keep things stirred up at the employee level in two ways. They refuse to deal with issues that require questioning or confronting any level of management above them, and they are constantly going above and beyond expectations, almost always at the expense of the front line, to please the boss above them.

On a day-to-day basis, the employees are frustrated and misused. The INQB has only one customer, his or her boss. If an employee comes to the INQB with a larger level problem that will impact customer satisfaction, the INQB will stall, divert attention from it, put pressure on the front-line employee to deal with it alone some way, or will let the problem persist but blame it on someone else. It is almost impossible for an INQB to confront his or her direct superiors with something unpleasant that might be potentially interpreted as criticism.

If the upper management institutes a policy or procedure that negatively impacts the employees who work for the INQB, the employees are without hope. Backing up employees would have a negative impact on the INQB. It won't happen.

Despite all of this careful accommodation, the INQB is always nervous about "the boss." Because of this, the INQB volunteers his or her employees for extra duty and in turn cranks up the expectations and pressures. In more severe cases, the boss hasn't even expressed a desire for something, but the INQB tries to anticipate and present it before the boss might request it. Of course, it is the front-line employees who do the extra work.

The INQB has usually earned the contempt of his or her employees. With the right spin in an autocratic organization, the INQB can turn that contempt into even more boss-pleasing collateral. After all, employees are expected to do as they are told. In some organizations, a whining front line is almost a feather in the manager's cap. The INQB easily becomes a key player. Other upper management will love the INQB because he is seen as handling problems effectively, and he doesn't pose a real threat to their own advancement potential.

Looking at the INQB is like viewing someone through a two-sided mirror. The management behind the INQB see only themselves. The unseen employees get the real picture.

The INQB's contribution in an organization can be compared to a museum filled with modern art. You can hang the picture upside down and perhaps nobody will notice, but still something is wrong.

Professional Strategy:

If you suspect you're an INQB:

- You probably don't suspect you're an INQB; you know it.
- Ask yourself what purpose it serves you to be unable to stand up for your employees, for yourself, or for better ideas. Be sure you at least know what you are bargaining away.
- Be aware that communication is probably poor between you and your employees. Seek ways to improve it.

If you are an employee:

- Don't question authority, your boss's or upper management's, in front of the INQB.
- Expect to produce and not make any comments or suggestions.
- Don't get hooked into emotion-charged conversations with the INQB. Keep things objective and professional.
- Don't try to rationalize your situation as normal. It is not.

If you manage an INQB:

- Encourage debate and involve the INQB in positive brainstorming.
- Ask direct questions that require the INQB to discuss the cons as well as the pros of a proposal. Show that disagreement is not disaster.
- The INQB often ends up creating an environment where employees become time clock punchers. Watch for it. You can lose dedicated employees even if they don't leave.

ITAC

I TAKE ALL THE CREDIT

"We're all in this alone."

Lily Tomlin
Comedienne and actress

The ITAC management style operates from the standpoint that because the manager takes the responsibility, he or she should also take the credit. It's a little like the old feudal lord formula. "You do the work and bring me the grain. I'll throw you a few crumbs when it's convenient." While this is a beneficial posture for the ITAC, it is detrimental to the rest of the organization.

People who work for an ITAC don't always catch on to what is happening. The ITAC is usually liberal with the pats on the back and makes the employee feel appreciated and valued. The employees are initially motivated to work hard and increase their contributions. This can work well for a long time if the ITAC is clever enough to keep the employees isolated so that they don't find out what happens to their work down the road.

The ITAC is truly a two-faced coin. The smiling appreciation lavished on the employees on one side is usually offset by a total disregard of their contributions on the other. To the rest of the organization, the attitude is that the manager conceived the good ideas and carefully shepherded the employees into bringing the project to fruition. The unspoken premise is that high quality projects are a direct result of good management rather than a result of good work by the employees. A particularly destructive ITAC will even accentuate the difficulties, or fabricate some, that had to be overcome to make the project come together. Observers will be left thinking how lucky for the organization that the ITAC was there to pull it all together.

You might ask what real harm this does. After all, at least the work is getting done. I think it does a great deal of harm. Any time something doesn't feel right, and this certainly doesn't, we need to take a hard look at it.

In the case of the ITAC, there are three very real costs.

The betrayal the employees feel when they discover they've been used is huge. It destroys trust and in some cases sets up an urge for retribution. That can only be harmful to the individuals involved and to the organization. Productivity will decline; there is no way around it.

The second is that the ITAC keeps all the upper management focus targeted on him or herself. Thus, other managers in the organization have no opportunity to get a feel for the talent pool on which the ITAC is floating. This severely limits the opportunity for those employees who work for the ITAC to advance or to even move laterally in the organization. They are treated as well-kept secrets. This might be flattering to the employees, but it's a sham that keeps them under control where they can benefit the ITAC. And, because the ITAC won't want his or her "people" to get too much individual recognition, you can be sure they won't be offered the training and development opportunities they probably deserve.

The third cost of the ITAC characteristic is in product quality. Typically, the ITAC organizes the information flow so that only he or she can ultimately put all the pieces together. While it's true that employees might do the lion's share of the work and might have had most of the good ideas, the ITAC will need to feel the sense of importance that comes with being the only one who can perform the final steps. Often, the ITAC creates pockets of people who are working on the same project but either keeps them separated or, worse yet, creates distrust between the groups to keep them from communicating. After all, if everyone involved on the project could communicate with the other participants, the entire project might be done without the leader. That would be unacceptable to the ITAC. Knowing this, one might ask, even if the results are okay under the ITAC, wouldn't they typically be better if information could flow freely in the group?

Professional Strategy:

If you believe the work your employees do is rightly yours, give yourself the following little quiz and see how you feel about your responses:

- If a salesperson put a product in your bag, but forgot to ring it up, would you keep it without paying for it?
- If you were standing in line at the post office and

the person in front of you dropped a ten dollar bill from their pocket, would you wait until they stepped away and then pick it up, or would you draw their attention to it?

- Is the word "ownership" the same for management and for the front-line employee?

If you work for or with an ITAC:

- ITACs are loyal only to themselves. Cover your bases. If a project blows up, the ITAC will point fingers.

- Recognize that the ITAC is a political animal. Protect yourself accordingly.

If you are an employee:

- Get to know people in the organization who do not work for the ITAC. Meet socially or seek out training opportunities. This will help you see how your work is being presented and will give you access to other areas of the organization.

If you manage an ITAC:

- Isolate projects or accomplishments you know were chiefly employee-driven and suggest the ITAC leave his or her name off of them.

- Model employee appreciation.

- Set up formal employee recognition procedures that force the ITAC to give a public pat on the back.

JPBH

JUST PLAIN BUTT HEAD

"These are the people who think they are doing what is
right when they aren't, and they do it with sustained gusto and
enthusiasm."

JD Taylor
Rear Admiral, US Navy, Ret.

There are many ways to describe someone who has this management characteristic: arrogant, narcissistic, mean, jerk, bully. I bet some of these folks are still carrying around the lunch money they pounded out of some poor kid in the fourth grade. We find these people at all levels of management, and unfortunately, the farther they advance, the worse they become. One JPBH I knew told me with a sense of pride that he considered each day a total loss unless he made someone mad. He said this with an arrogant smile and he meant it.

I've always wondered how JPBHs get their advancements. With some of them, I can only suspect blackmail, but others probably steamrolled whoever stood in their way and elbowed their way into the new position. JPBHs learn early that people will do almost anything to get them out of their face, and it makes it easy for them to get what they want.

As a rule, people cannot thrive in a caustic environment, yet that is exactly what JPBHs produce. They are masters of finding the weak psychological link in everyone they encounter and they pounce on it. "If you're going to win, win big time; don't pussyfoot around with people's feelings," they say to themselves, and their justification for nearly everything is, "Because I want it, that's why."

JPBHs like to see people cower. "If they're afraid of me," they reason, "they'll work better." I wouldn't want most JPBHs to baby-sit my dog, yet organization after organization lets people like this inflict a daily dose of emotional pain on the people they employ.

As with many of the other destructive management characteristics, upper management often misses the mark by allowing the JPBH to remain in the job. Of course, from the upper management side, the JPBH might be a bit rough or a little bit caustic, but they don't see the damage that is being caused down the line. They don't see it, because they won't look.

JPBHs are very bright. Those who employ them find them invaluable in sheer brain power and are therefore willing to overlook some of their failings. JPBHs know this and use it to justify their own behavior. Their intellect becomes a weapon instead of a gift, and anyone who might want to check a JPBH's behavior quickly learns that it's easier to avoid the issue.

Leaders must look carefully at the people to whom they give power. In small roles, JPBHs are jerks, perhaps, but the offenses are usually relatively small. People who aren't being stung personally might even find the JPBH amusing. They laugh at the gall of the person. But be wary, the JPBHs who can work the most evil will also be the hardest to nail down. They will hide behind policies and regulations and will justify their destructive behavior with impeccable logic. You might not be fooled, but you won't have grounds for action, either. Advancing a JPBH in error can be an expensive nightmare. Over time, his or her behavior will give the company an above average chance of being sued, or it will create a collective bargaining crisis. And it is all preventable.

Professional Strategy:

If you suspect you are Just a Plain Butt Head:

- You probably are if you think the world is a stage, and you are the only real actor on it.
- You probably aren't if you've read this far without being forced.

If you work for or with a JPBH:

- Be careful about crossing a JPBH. They have long memories and love a good payback.
- Don't expect normal responses to emotional situations. You can't predict a JPBH's behavior.

If you are an employee:

- If it's certain that upper management won't be eliminating the problem, get a new job. Leave. You deserve better. Find someplace to thrive, because you can't thrive working for one of these people.

If you manage a JPBH:

- Be very sure this person is irreplaceable. Otherwise, you owe it to the employees and your organization to think about replacing him or her.
- Don't let a JPBH prevail in disagreements with you just because he or she becomes unpleasant. Remember, you're the supervisor.

MBFOM
MANAGEMENT BY FLAVOR OF THE MONTH

"If you don't know where you're going, any path will take you there."
Sioux Proverb

The MBFOMs are the kings and queens of good intentions. They want so much to do the right thing the right way that they've turned their personal compasses off and are blown in whatever direction the prevailing winds of current thinking might dictate. They are training seminar junkies, and while their constantly renewed enthusiasms are perhaps laudable, the effect on everyone who must constantly react to a new structure or new procedure or new language is negative.

Here is yet another example of a good quality taken to detrimental extremes. Nobody can fault the MBFOM for wanting to implement new ideas and to keep abreast of modern management theory, but the underlying shortcoming that lurks behind this knee-jerk fad adoption must be examined and the costs of allowing it to occur must be calculated.

Sometimes I think of MBFOMs as the professional students of the management world. They love to study and they love to sit in class and get excited about a theory or an idea. The problem is that they can't get out of the starting blocks and successfully carry any of these approaches to fruition. Either they don't have the skills to lead employees into true change or they are too soon distracted by the next great idea for the last one to have a chance. Instead of leading, they seem to be jumping from pond to pond, flailing until the water is muddy enough that they need to jump to another.

The MBFOMs shine the most, at least in their own eyes, when they are expounding on philosophies and ideas. They are usually well read on organizational and management topics and love to talk the talk, yet they are unable to formulate the concrete steps it would take to make anything really work. They want everything to be nice and for everyone around them to just get it, making these wonderful feel-good visions an automatic reality. It never quite happens.

Undaunted, the MBFOM attends another seminar that no doubt holds the key, and meantime there is no real work getting done. The employees left behind are enjoying the break from the "noise" the MBFOM adds to the work environment, but at the same time are bracing themselves for the inevitable series of meetings and memos and new procedures that will be announced upon the boss's return. They know that sending the boss to a seminar is like sending a terrorist to an ammo bunker for a two-day shopping trip.

The employees know what's going on. They feel that the MBFOM can't really lead and so is creating a mask or is grasping at straws. If you put it up to a vote the, MBFOM would get "no confidence." The employees might appreciate the intent, but they resent the waste of their talent and energy. If the seminars happen to result in a shorter work week for the manager, an excuse to sleep late on Monday, or company paid pseudo-work to exotic locations, the manager will inevitably be despised. What is sad about this is that MBFOMs are almost always really nice people.

It would be bad enough if the cost to an organization was limited to the cost of the MBFOM's salary and benefits, but the MBFOMs cost much more than that. Productivity is a word with almost no meaning for the MBFOM and therefore, the employees will have trouble seeing the point of exertion. Nothing they do counts, everything is transient, there is no leadership. Here again, there is room to expect the worst for the organization. There can be no loyalty where there is no respect.

As a final comment, let me point out that I give seminars and do management consulting for a living. I believe passionately in what I do, and maybe I'll lose money by giving you this advice, but if you have an MBFOM, find other work for them, perhaps, but don't send them to any more seminars. Don't let them sign up! Just Say No.

Professional Strategy:

If you believe you might be an MBFOM:

- Know that you are probably a good-hearted soul. That doesn't mean you will be a good manager. Examine this carefully.

- Come to terms with the reality that while it is wonderful to work *with* you, it is probably difficult to work *for* you.

- Examine what you really enjoy about your profession. If it's helping people, God bless you, but perhaps you aren't in the right field. Helping skills and leading skills often go hand in hand, but not always. Find the place where you can best make a difference. You deserve to flourish. Find an area where you can grow.

- Honestly assess whether your skills and interests are a good match for your current job. Going to a seminar to work on your weaknesses will not help you. If you want to stay where you are, find a mentor within the organization who is not like you, but who empathizes and appreciates your sensibilities.

If you are an employee:

- God bless you, too, for your patience!

- Recognize that any real leadership in your department is probably being done covertly by the staff. Find out what the system is and decide whether you can afford the risk of joining it.

- If the MBFOM is giving vague emotion-charged directions, firmly, yet gently, demand specifics. You might have to help him or her by offering suggestions as examples, but at least you'll be able to move forward.

- Don't get attached to any one project or methodology. If you thrive on order and consistency, consider looking for another job. This one will make you crazy.

- From a security point of view, it might be wise to take notes and keep a file of directions you receive when you suspect they will be countermanded later. Generally, nobody likes to get an MBFOM fired— after all, he or she could be replaced by a Just Plain Butt Head—but situations can arise where facts stated by a clear head can be vital.

If you manage an MBFOM:

- Watch for projects and plans that never quite reach completion. If there are too many of them, guide the MBFOM through evaluating the causes of the stalls.

- Help the MBFOM jettison the activities that are not fruitful. All of those seminars and books can spawn a lot of procedures and programs. Look at which ones are working and which ones are wasting time.

- Discuss current projects or issues and negotiate with the MBFOM what the approach will be for that project or for a specific period of time. Insist that the approach be adhered to until completion.

- Be wary about sending the MBFOM to any training seminars that might launch a new tangent. Even personal productivity seminars are dangerous.

MBLOL
MANAGEMENT BY LENGTH OF THE LEASH

"If you've got them by the balls,

their hearts and minds will soon follow."

Charles Colson
Special Assistant to President Richard Nixon
The Watergate tapes, 1974

What's the first thing some dogs do when you put them on a leash? They go right out to the end of it and start pulling. For MBLOL types, that's what management feels like to them. They are the ones holding the leash, and their job is to teach those employees, perhaps even humanely, to stop pulling the leash and to heel without being told.

The Utopian vision for the MBLOL manager is everyone at their desk, doing the same thing quietly, and doing it by the book. To really be perfect, everyone would look the same, too.

For the MBLOL, management is about numbers, order, and control, not about people. Everything must be quantified and directed. To the MBLOL, if somebody doesn't walk the line just right, the entire order of things could collapse. The zeal with which the pigeonholes are designed, built, maintained, tidied up, and classified, illustrates that for the MBLOL, stringency is not only desirable, it is a matter of survival. MBLOLs find interpersonal communication stressful, employee problems messy, and at some deep level, the customer a necessary evil.

Life is black and white to the MBLOL. Something is either done properly or it is bad for the company. There isn't much room for interpretation, and there certainly isn't room for creativity or independent thinking. For an MBLOL, information management is a structured approach to accountability. It's all down on paper, we can't argue with the numbers, and if your number happens to be in the wrong column, bye-bye.

It seems obvious that this type of manager would be undesirable in a company. After all, where is the dynamic for better ways of doing things? Where is the place for productive non-conformity? How do employees prepare to assume leadership when their daily workload is mapped out to the smallest detail?

MBLOLs persist, however, because, regardless of the terms in which their employees might discuss them, other management will see them as people whose departments run like clockwork. Their areas buzz with people at work, people who are focused on the task at hand. "No surprises" feels like good management sometimes. Unfortunately, the fact that the employees are drying up, heart and soul, and aren't giving anything extra to the company doesn't register on the reports. It registers in the organization's overall health, but it's difficult to lay the blame at the feet of the MBLOL. MBLOLs can kill the company, but the death is slower than with other destructive styles and the cause could be masked by other, more obvious, problems.

Because MBLOLs are good at instilling order, they might be

good at restructuring problem areas, but you can't leave them in any one position for too long. MBLOLs burn out employees with their rigidity. Morale, creativity, communication and loyalty are subject to assault from the MBLOL behavior. MBLOLs are like powerful prescription drugs. They might get the job done, but the side effects can be awful.

Professional Strategy:

If you think you Manage By the Length of the Leash:

- Realize that while your intentions are good, you could be doing real damage to your organization.
- Ask if you really enjoy the kind of work you do. There are many respected careers where you can sit quietly at a desk, do your work, and not be bothered by the rat race. Evaluate what is keeping you from finding such a career for yourself. Maybe you need a change.
- Recognize the worth of value systems other than your own. Part of the problem might be that you don't appreciate different styles of learning, communication, and organization.

If you work for or with an MBLOL:

- It is unlikely that they'll see a problem with their style. The ends justify the means in their book.
- Trying to change this environment is like beating your head against a wall. Don't do it; you'll get a headache.

If you are an employee:

- Do your work impeccably. Find out what "the right way" is to the MBLOL and do it that way whenever possible. Even seemingly small things like organizing with binders instead of with files, if that is their preference, can go a long way with an MBLOL.

- If you find yourself feeling confined by the leash, it might be time to run away. Learn what you can where you are, then find a new opportunity where you can roam more freely.

If you manage an MBLOL:

- Attend departmental meetings and observe the dynamics. Are employees free to interject? Are new ideas welcomed? Is the meeting too heavy on communicating policies and strict procedures?

- Watch the department attrition rate. If it's high, be sure to get exit interviews and address specific issues that arise.

- Invest in training that focuses on understanding differences in how people perceive and process input.

MDOF
MY DOOR IS OPEN TO FAVORITES

"A closed door policy not only shuts you [the manager] in, it shuts out the career growth path of those who can benefit from you."
Jack Most
Former General Council, Revlon

MDOFs struggle with insecurity. Their only method for assuring comfort in a job is to surround themselves with cronies who will always pat them on the back and be loyal supporters. It's a bit of a war for MDOFs. They need the inner circle to form a ring of wagons to protect them from the rest of the employees.

You can spot MDOFs a mile away. They are big on open door policies, but when their close friends and "wannabe's" are crowded into the office, often several times a day, there is almost a party atmosphere. Employees outside the inner circle find themselves having to interrupt the gaiety to ask business questions in front of the entire group. This is not to say that managers can't have friendships and engage in casual conversations with employees. The problem is when it is carried to a destructive extreme, or when the door is open to chosen employees and closed to the rest.

With the MDOF, quality of work has no bearing on who gets privileges, whose ideas are given consideration, and who is treated with respect instead of cold indifference. It is management by personality. If the manager likes someone, that person is "in." If not, he or she is tolerated or simply "out." If insecurity is at the root of this behavior, and I believe it is, it isn't surprising that the most qualified and talented employees are typically left hanging out to dry while those who drag the productivity of the group into the basement become the boss's pets. MDOFs can spot people with no backbone or self-worth a mile away and will quickly draw them into their circle. They certainly aren't going to surround themselves with someone who has enough self-confidence not to play the game.

The destructive effect of this management style should be clear. Obviously, the employees who are kept on the outside will be frustrated and demoralized. Worse yet, they won't trust the employees on the inside. You end up with two distinct camps and a lot of hard feelings. A team environment has little chance with this management behavior. While it isn't the organization's job to ensure "good feelings" for employees, employees are entitled to at least minimal professionalism from their bosses. Even employees who state a desire to "just come to work and do my job," will not be able to exempt themselves from the political whirlpool an MDOF creates. The inner circle will know everything the boss knows about everyone's personal issues or work challenges. The people in the inside circle will become increasingly less productive and those on the outside will have to shoulder the burden. The work atmosphere will become more toxic by the day and eventually the real contributors will wise up and leave. By that point, the ship will be sinking and the costs will have already been tallied on the financial statements.

Upper management, however, might have a hard time spotting the problem. They might work closely with the MDOF to treat the symptoms, but it won't occur to them that the problem originated with the MDOF. After all, a quick glance shows that he or she has an excellent rapport with the staff. There are a lot of smiling people in the department. People who struggled in the past appear to have blossomed under the MDOF tutelage. Unless upper management is willing to seek out and talk with the front-line workers who aren't buddies with the boss, the organization will never know what hit them. And, potentially more damaging, they might become convinced that an open door policy and the "feel good fluff" people promote as good management simply doesn't work.

Professional Strategy:

If you suspect you are a MDOF:

- You might have become an MDOF in all innocence. Forgive yourself, but change your ways.
- It isn't necessary to like your employees equally or for them to like you, but you need to treat them equally. If some people have trouble getting respectful access to you, your door isn't really open.

If you are an employee:

- Realize that these special relationships are a form of power for the MDOF. It isn't going to change.
- Beware of telling an MDOF anything of a confidential nature. The inside scoop is the medium of trade for the MDOF.
- Figure out the pecking order as early as possible. Recognize that there is probably a lot of deceit going on around you. Stay above it.
- As much as possible, go with the flow. Choose to be a positive example of adult behavior in an environment that's been regressed to the junior high level.

If you manage an MDOF:

- Help the MDOF map out strategies to break down barriers in the department. Set a structure for the MDOF. A regular brown-bag lunch, team-building activities, even a lunch potluck will help the department personalities mix a little better.
- Insist that the manager engage in a one-on-one status check with each member of the department on a regular basis. Weekly is ideal. This can be quick and informal, but the environment must encourage employee input.
- Attend meetings within the department and help the MDOF to see if non-favorites appear to be discounted.

MNOE
My Name is On Everything

"Those who bow to the man above will always step on the man below."

Dagobert D. Runes
Editor, publisher, philosopher

For some people, there is something nourishing to the soul about seeing their name in print. For them, even writing it gives them a little thrill. While this might be true of all of us to some degree, the MNOE has taken it to the degree of fetish. For the MNOE, self-worth lies in the number of memos, letters, contracts, and forms he or she had to sign in a given day. It's a measure of productivity. The more signatures required, the more important the MNOE must be. For an MNOE, a chance to meet with the boss and report that he or she "sent out the Freebish memo and the Dinkfarb contracts" is reward beyond measure.

In and of itself, this characteristic isn't destructive in the way the other seventeen management behaviors are. As long as it doesn't get in the way of getting the work done, which is a real danger, let the MNOE have his or her thrills while everyone else keeps the wheels turning. Even a good manager can have this little hang-up, but it's worth looking a little deeper to be sure that the MNOE doesn't also exhibit one of the other more destructive characteristics. The same urge that causes this obsession can be the birthplace of some of the others. And, if taken to the extreme, the MNOE obsession can affect the morale of the organization and hinder productivity.

It's easy to poke fun at MNOEs, and their employees certainly do. The most common setup for derision is the Certificate of Recognition. Don't get me wrong, in some situations such certificates symbolize achievement that is worthy of recognition and honor. In those cases, the corporate culture values and supports this formal pat on the back. The MNOE likes to hand out certificates wholesale, however, harboring the illusion that the employee will look at the certificate on the wall and tearfully feel both motivated and inspired by the sight of the boss's signature. I can imagine the great satisfaction with which the MNOE practices writing his or her signature before carefully signing each certificate.

Granted, there are some folks out there who will buy frames and display every little certificate they've ever received. I've seen offices and cubicles with so many awards and certificates that it looks like a storage locker for the National Archives. These folks will love the MNOE style, but they are in the minority.

If the MNOE has other management weaknesses, it will be difficult for the employees who work under him or her to maintain any level of respect. The MNOE will look like a fool and productivity will plummet. In this way, the MNOE can be as expensive as the other types of managers who are missing the mark.

Professional Strategies:

If you suspect you are an MNOE:

- This one little quirk doesn't necessarily mean you aren't a good manager. It is entirely possible, however, that you are wasting important time and resources and that you could be more productive if you could wean yourself of this habit.
- Make a list of all the documents you encounter during a two-day period. Which were really necessary, and of those, which really required your review and signature?

If you work for or with an MNOE:

- Recognize that these people are paper-driven. They can support a good idea, but they need to get input in paper form. Give it to them.
- Recognize that you might have a bit more bureaucracy to wade through with this manager, but try to evaluate him or her with a larger view. An MNOE can be a great leader or a lousy one.

If you are an employee:

- If you're fighting to survive, bury him or her in your paper production. If you create a draft report, include a cover page that says: "Submitted to:" with his name and the date. Ask for her signature on things whenever possible or ask her to initial things to "cover" small issues. She will like you better for it.

MODC
Master Of Damage Control

"There is no situation that cannot be made more difficult with just a little bit of effort."

David Gerrold, Author

You can spot MODCs by their reactive nature. They are masters at sniffing out the projects which are teetering on the edge of destruction and fixing the problems. They are usually willing to take the heat when their attempts at resuscitation fail, and they are often intensely loyal to the organization. In some cases, God bless the MODCs, they often keep the organization afloat by simply plugging the "leaks" in the organizational ship.

A MODC can sometimes do good work as a public relations officer. MODCs are usually fast thinkers, and if they are able to keep the big picture and the party line in view, they can often save a rotting fish. Being a MODC, of course, does not guarantee the expression of any other qualities, so I give that example by way of illustration only. If a MODC is missing a strong ethic, his or her reactive impulses can spell big trouble. I once saw a MODC give an agency director false information out of blind loyalty to the department in which he was employed. The MODC was operating out of patronage, not principle, and in this case, the resulting misunderstandings and repercussions were devastating.

It is this impulse to "make the save no matter what" that is both the gift and the curse of the MODC. If they have tight rein on their impulses, they can be extremely valuable to an organization when employed appropriately.

The major cause for concern is that a MODC might do a great job in an emergency, but is probably a poor manager on a sustained basis. MODCs abhor long-term strategic planning, they thrive on crisis, and they can't stay away from the scene of other people's disasters.

Unfortunately, because organizations often have an impulse of gratitude after a good save, MODCs are often given regular management positions as a reward. When this happens, they are more likely to create havoc than to tame it, and because they are more concerned with a hastily-constructed fix, they usually overlook the underlying cause of the problems they try to solve in their new role. They are constantly trying to catch the wagging tail.

This, of course, is confusing to the upper management who advanced them. "They managed situation *We're Going Under* so well," they say to themselves. "Why don't those same qualities work in situation *Daily Grind?*"

Everyone must work on damage control sometimes. That's life. And being good at it is important. Again, it is when the ability to function well in one situation gets a person into a situation in which they don't really belong. Some people are well-rounded and can be managers and work on damage control at the same time. MODCs, however, are the extreme case. It is unfair to fence them in. They will hate the fences as much as those inside the fence will come to hate them.

Professional Strategy:

If you think you might be a MODC:

- Don't take advancements that will make you miserable.

- You might need to create your own title and function. Maintain your maverick freedom and make your best contribution to the organization. Think it through carefully, and sell it to the right people at the right time.

- Recognize that you are both creative and reactive. The corporate world might try to take your round peg thinking and cram it into a square hole. You need to take an honest look at your abilities, and if you want to give longer-term management assignments a try, recognize that you'll need to develop some new habits to make it work.

- Find a mentor to help you develop specific upstream thinking strategies. If you find a complementary personality, you can help him or her with the brush fires, and you can get help with the plowing.

If you work with or for a MODC:

- He or she is probably feeling as frustrated as you are. It might help to know that.
- MODCs are reactive by nature. It's a great relief to know you can run to them in a crisis, because they don't lose their heads in panic. It's unsettling to know that they often have a hand, unintentionally, in creating the crisis in the first place.

If you are an employee:

- If you like structure and direction, you'll have to calculate how long you can last in the chaos and then figure out whether you are likely to outlast your boss.

If you manage a MODC:

- Mentor him or her—through modeling and direct guidance—into longer-range thinking. MODCs are usually very bright.

SFVA
Searching for Value-Added

"When you give advice, remember that Socrates was a Greek philosopher who went around giving good advice. They poisoned him."

Anonymous

Some people simply must leave their mark. It's a natural human desire, but in the case of the SFVA, it's a case of personal need overwhelming wisdom and practicality. The SFVA is the guy who reviews sales quotes and insists on changing an inconsequential detail after all the paperwork has already been completed. It's the woman who makes the creator of a presentation change the entire thing because she doesn't like the background.

While it's true that small details are often important and that the wrong images in a presentation can make it less effective, the motivation behind the changes with an SFVA is not always an improvement of the end product, but the need to see his or her input acted upon.

How do we tell the difference between someone who is dedicated to making the project better and someone who is an SFVA? Over time, it's pretty easy. Watch the reaction of the dedicated employees—if there are any left—who work in the department. An SFVA is resented because his or her suggestions are viewed as thinly disguised power plays and the implementation of the suggestions is seen as a waste of time. In management meetings where consensus is important, SFVAs refuse to let anything reach a conclusion until they've had their input accepted and integrated.

People who work with the SFVA find themselves frustrated and then kicking themselves because they buy into the premise that the SFVA is just trying to make things better. In reality, SFVAs are just trying to *feel* better.

It doesn't take a lot of imagination to see that a chronic SFVA can send productivity down the drain. It's expensive to repeatedly send people back to the drawing board after they've done the bulk of the work, and it's terrible for morale.

It must be noted that there are managers who find themselves at the end of the review process who really must ask for changes that create expense and extra work. Notice, however, that the suggestions of these managers are often met with a grateful "thank goodness you noticed that" or at least a grudging "you're right, I'll fix it." The manager weighs the cost of the change against his or her opinion that the change would improve the end result, and sometimes lets things stand "as is." Leaders insisting on a change near the end of the process recognize the work that has been done and don't devalue it by petty and haphazard alterations. For them, changes are dictated from experience and wisdom, not from a need to see that they affect outcomes.

When we look at the SFVA in this light, we can see the insecurity that drives the behavior. A leader rejoices when a team does great work without too much of his or her direct input. An SFVA feels left out.

To bolster his or her position, especially in management-heavy organizations, an SFVA will often try to create self-doubt in others. This constant need to undermine confidence can be subtle, but deadly. When a team becomes convinced they aren't able to do a job well, it won't be long before they prove it.

SFVAs are surprisingly plentiful in the workplace. When you know something is amiss, but haven't quite put your finger on it, this behavior somewhere in the organization could easily be part of the problem. It's another behavior to which we've become numb, and it can take a tremendous cut from the bottom line.

Professional Strategy:

If you think you might be an SFVA:

- You're probably in shock, because you hadn't realized what you were doing.
- Be kind to yourself, you are not alone.
- Get in the habit of asking yourself every time you start to make a suggestion why you are making it and what it will cost.
- Take more care to respect the energies and output of the people around you. Everyone needs to shine. Leaders let them.

If you work for or with an SFVA:

- Take the approach that this is a bad habit and that it might be fixable. It might not be, but at least begin with that assumption.

If you are an employee:

- When planning your time, leave room for the inevitable last minute changes. They will still annoy you, but at least they won't put you off schedule.

If you manage the SFVA:

- Have a heart-to-heart talk and work out a method for changing the behavior. Sometimes just an awareness of the problem can help.
- If the problem is particularly bad, select some situations and require that the SFVA document what he or she calculates as the cost of the suggested changes and weigh them against the estimated return.

STATTS
STAND THERE AND TAKE IT TO SURVIVE

"The trouble with Archie is, he don't know how to worry without getting upset."

Edith Bunker
All In The Family, 1970s

This destructive management behavior is best described by what the employees have to do as a result of it. They have to stand there and take it as their manager shouts at them or others in an angry tirade.

STATTS managers use anger as a weapon. There is tremendous power for them in using words, and maybe even explosive gestures, to make an employee wither. It means the employee will do what is wanted in the future. The louder the volume, the better. The point will be made and remembered.

This must be what STATTS tell themselves to rationalize behavior that has no place in the workplace, or in fact as it is often seen, anywhere. STATTS are simply out of control. They've bottled up their frustrations to the point that they have to explode somewhere and at someone.

We all have bad days. We all lose our tempers, but STATTS jump to that level of anger with regularity. As they wind up, they begin blaming others for their own errors and often find the most emotionally vulnerable employees to use as verbal whipping posts.

The effect of all this, even if it only occurs three or four times a year, is that the emotional lift that induces creativity, enthusiasm, and productivity is replaced by a sickened feeling that sticks to the atmosphere like cigarette smoke on clothing. People who are hurt, frightened, or angry, aren't going to contribute their best work. The emotional factors in such an environment become so overwhelming that the focus of the daily grind is not about the work, the product, or the customer; it's about the interpersonal dynamic between the STATTS and the employees. People who might normally be bringing a project to completion are instead picking up the emotional pieces for the victim of the latest STATTS outburst. Resentment is a destructive energy in the workplace. It works consistent and far-reaching mischief. It is the logical by-product of witnessing such behavior, let alone being the target of it.

Professional Strategy:

If you think you might be a STATTS:

- You wouldn't be this angry if you didn't have something to be angry about. Get some help and find out what it really is instead of flashing in anger at people and situations that don't merit that response.
- Work hard to direct your anger at situations. Leave individuals out of it. Nobody is company property and nobody is being paid to be demeaned.

- Recognize that your outbursts are inflicting damage on people and on the organization.
- It might surprise you to learn that weathering these kinds of emotional storms is not a part of everybody's background. These rages are totally alien to many people and they will not be able to brush them off as you might expect. It does not make them wimps.

If you work for or with a STATTS:

- Keep in mind that the anger and shouting probably have nothing to do with you. The STATTS is grasping for someone and something to vent about, and the more off-base the accusations, the more emphatic the venting will be.
- Try to remain emotionally detached from the tirades. The STATTS will lash out in any direction to find a weak spot to hit. Know that this is happening and don't buy into it.
- Tread softly and keep your bases covered.
- Recognize that STATTS often interpret questions about or objections to their ideas as direct accusations that they are not good enough at their job. Don't be surprised when the reaction far exceeds the stimulus. STATTS can be highly qualified, talented people, and they often have good hearts. They might be as baffled by their behavior as you are.

If you manage a STATTS:

- Deal with the problem directly. Explain that you cannot tolerate such destructive outbursts. If the person has many offsetting qualities, it is easy to be supportive of the person and intolerant of the behavior. Offer help.
- If the behavior doesn't change—even if you feel you must keep the STATTS in the company—at least change the structure to get the employees out of the line of fire.

TMIB

Trust Me, I'm the Boss

"There comes a time in the affairs of man when he must take the bull by the tail and face the situation."

William Claude (W.C.) Fields
American comedian and film star

TMIBs are hung up on decision making. To the TMIB, he or she is the boss, and therefore the responsibility for making decisions is his or hers. The only problem is that TMIBs have trouble making decisions. They start out right and gather information. Then they gather information and gather information and gather information.

When pressed for a decision, they say the responsibility is theirs and to trust them. They'll get back to you. Then they rush out and try to build a consensus opinion so they know what their decision should be. Somehow, it doesn't seem they can do their job justice unless they have reached a point of being overwhelmed. They have to make everything agonizing and even after having made the decision, they agonize on when to tell it to someone.

TMIBs often don't know where they stand. They hide behind their title and use it to buy time. They are masters of generating a smoke screen to justify their procrastination. Meanwhile, the decision looms ever larger to them, and often is becoming more pressing to those who need to know what the decision will be. The stakes go up and the expressions of anxiety are met with, "Trust me, I'll take care of it."

You can tell the employees of a TMIB because they are all bald from pulling their hair out. Well, at least figuratively. They are exasperated. They are trapped between the rock of a pressing need and the immovable object that is their boss.

The TMIBs are often well-meaning, good people. They don't realize that as they systematically go through their process, that people around them are having spikes in their blood pressure. The fact that they have the title should provide the employees some reassurance, they think, while at the same time they are frozen in indecision. Apart from potentially destructive pressure the employees must endure unnecessarily, TMIBs are dangerous to a company because the potential for missed opportunity is high and problem situations are allowed to fester too long before action is taken.

Professional Strategy:

If you think you might be a TMIB:

- TMIBs usually dislike decision-making in their personal lives, too. If you have problems in this area in general, you might be compensating by being a TMIB.
- Analyze the types of decisions you are making and delegate some of them to your employees as appropriate. Chances are, you are over-managing in

some respects. Reserve your decision-making angst for the issues that really require your involvement.

If you work for or with a TMIB:

- Try to anticipate your own needs. If you see a problem coming, get it in front of the TMIB as early as possible. It might change the order in which you perform your tasks, but it will probably make you more efficient in the long run, because you'll have a better chance of having the information you need sooner.

- You'll need to be a squeaky wheel, but you'll have to be careful about how and when you squeak. You don't want to pressure the TMIB into burying the problem completely.

If you manage a TMIB:

- You might be snowed by the show of confidence. Check for results.

- Put the TMIB into roles where the decision-making is more routine.

- When asked for input, talk through the decision-making process with the TMIB, when possible, rather than just stating your conclusion. Teach the process.

WIIFM

WHAT'S IN IT FOR ME

"Far too many executives have become concerned with the
"four P's"—pay, perks, power and prestige —rather than making
profits for shareholders."

T. Boone Pickens, Jr.
1988

Those who enter into a contract with the workplace owe it to themselves and their families to be sure the contract is fair. "What's in it for me?" is a legitimate and important question. Without it, we become the golden geese of the corporate worlds. In exchange for some cheap grain, we make somebody else wealthy.

On the other hand, we all know that once in the workplace, the tendency is to become invested. We form relationships with team members and, if we're lucky, we find a worthwhile purpose in the mission of the work. The good-hearted amongst us will do a job well because it's our job to do so. We owe it to ourselves to be kind, to be supportive, and to do our best.

WIIFMs don't work under the same set of values. They are political animals in the worst sense. They can smile to your face, talk cooperation and teamwork, and when you're not looking, pull the rug out from under you if it's to their benefit to do so. WIIFMs have one loyalty, to themselves. They will speak and act loyally until your back is against the wall, then they'll attack with the rest of the pack.

To be supervised by a WIIFM is to be the equivalent of a draft horse or ox. Work, pull, keep your nose down and produce, because if you don't, the WIIFM will look bad. WIIFMs are quick to take the credit and quicker to shift the blame. They do things for others to manipulate them, rarely because it is the right thing to do. If you need something from your WIIFM, you'd better hope it doesn't inconvenience him or her.

Sooner or later, despite all the smiles and good talk, the WIIFM will show his or her true colors. It is difficult to expect people to rally behind such a person and to work as a team. The company will surely lose big time with this person sucking all the oxygen out of the corporate air.

I imagine the warning signs are there for upper management to see, if they'll only look. This is the person who always wants more money, more time off, or more recognition without having to do anything extra. WIIFMs are so convinced that they deserve all that they request, that sometimes they can convince others to see things the same way. They are usually very low on empathy and short on patience where their employees are concerned, but will go to all lengths to get in good with the upper management, greasing the skids for taking more out of the company later.

Professional Strategy:

If you suspect you might be a WIIFM:

- Analyze your motivations for the majority of daily tasks. In what ways do you give back to the world in a selfless way?
- Ask yourself what you need to feel good about yourself. Then ask yourself if that's what you would like your personal and professional integrity to be based upon.

If you work for or with a WIIFM:

- Don't buy into any declarations about your best interest. Always look at what else might be out there, driving the WIIFM. If he or she is courting you as an ally, try to figure out why and don't expect any loyalty in return. The WIIFM needs your talent to look good.
- WIIFMs respond to one thing: power. Remember that, and you'll avoid a lot of trouble.

If you are an employee:

- If you recognize the motivations, you can barter a bit more effectively. For example, looking good to the other managers can be a reward for the WIIFM. If you can put your request in the context of looking better than the other managers, you'll probably get what you want.

Conclusion

It's no secret that some of the styles we've looked at here are more destructive than others. The important point is, however, that they are all, indeed, destructive. They harm people, they harm productivity and, even if they don't suck the lifeblood out of a company as they often do, they are expensive.

Why has upper management let these conditions persist? In part, it is because the leadership is often on a short-term please-the-stockholders-this-quarter program themselves. It is perceived as more expedient to get an acceptable job done in the short term than to invest in a program of more lasting value. Also, I think our culture has, up to now, accepted these styles as a normal part of doing business.

I suggest that we stop looking the other way and confront these problems head on. Apart from addressing problem managers on a case-by-case basis, leadership must also commit to an ongoing program that changes destructive mindsets in the corporate culture. This includes looking at how managers are hired and investing in regular management training.

We need to keep our ears and eyes open and actively gather feedback that will alert us to developing problems so they can be addressed early and perhaps without negative effects on the parties involved. Leaders must teach their managers to lead and must continually model positive leadership. Help the managers to help the front line succeed.

WE PLAY EMPLOYEES AGAINST EACH OTHER UNDER

THE NOTION THAT NOT THE BEST, BUT THE LOYAL,

WILL BENCHMARK PERFORMANCE.

IDENTIFYING AND ELIMINATING THE FIEFDOMS

WITHIN THE COMPANY COULD BE THE MOST IMPORTANT

ORGANIZATIONAL TASK YOUR COMPANY FACES.

LIFE IN THE
CORPORATE FIEFDOM

"When two men in business always agree one of them is unnecesary."
William Wrigley, Jr.
Founder and President Wrigley & Company

The fundamental need of any organization and its employees is leadership. Without a strong sense of direction and a clear company ethic, the spiritual essence of a company slowly ebbs away. Instead of being a unified force of creativity and labor, the company becomes a loosely connected group of separate organizational cultures, all with separate goals and business styles. It becomes a series of fiefdoms.

These unspoken territories may or may not appear on any organizational chart. Fiefdoms can be pockets of political identity, management philosophies, certain jobs or other special interests. They can represent a small tear in the corporate fabric, or the problem can be widespread, occurring at every level. They can result from a rigidly-enforced structure or from weak managers who need to feel like lords of an empire. Fiefdoms can be formed intentionally, with the best motivations, or they can form as a result of destructive management styles. Any time there is competition, fear, or a breakdown of communication within a company, there is a fiefdom in place somewhere.

Many of our traditional work units lend themselves to becoming fiefdoms. They discourage people from communicating or sharing information. People attend meetings, but do not speak their minds. Individual sections are judged and evaluated by their individual outcomes and performance measures. It's every group for itself. The troubling part is that too often nobody sees these fiefdoms as a problem or even recognizes that these fiefdoms exist.

The costs of letting a company go the way of fiefdom are high. Let's take a look at how fiefdoms manifest themselves in a company and compare it with what *can be.*

INTRACOMPANY COMPETITION AND COMMUNICATION

Fiefdoms often thrive on having employees, work units, teams and sections competing with one another for better production. The competition can be formal or unspoken. It can be based on jealousy or it can be company-sanctioned, internally well-publicized contests.

However the competition arises, loyalty quickly shifts to the work unit and no longer lies with the company as a whole. Ideas that might benefit another group are left unspoken because another team's success results in a perceived loss of prestige to one's own team.

Whenever a group is deprived of the opportunity to benefit from another group's creativity or information, the entire enterprise suffers. It doesn't matter if it's at the management level or at the front line.

However it's structured, competition like this is misguided and originates from a place of weakness. It comes from managers needing all of the resources available to them directed to their personal success in the company.

They've fallen prey to the Getting The Gold Star Syndrome. You see, the group with the key information gets noticed and gets the funding. Whether formally or informally, they get the gold star. Who wouldn't put getting a gold star ahead of the larger, more vague corporate good?

As a side benefit, the Gold Star group can assure themselves that even if the product (or company) fails, at least they did their job well, and everyone else thinks they did so, too. Ironically, it can be that the very structure which created the gold star mentality contributed to its failure.

Gold star organizations, where each of the specific work units is judged on separate numbers and goals, are operating under a most dysfunctional principle: If you maximize the parts, and have employees compete against each other, you will automatically maximize the whole. This is absolute nonsense. Management will get the numbers they want and will look good on paper, but is that the goal of the company—to make the lords look good? Or, is it to turn out the best products and services for the price?

REFUSING TO PAY THE TRIBUTES

What happens to the serfs who won't play the game? If a unit or section doesn't get any award at all, or chooses not to participate in either the formal or the power-based game-playing, how is that perceived in the company culture? They are branded as not being team players. They aren't conforming and, there-fore, cannot be trusted. What it really means is that they're play-ing by a different set of internal rules.

This team might not be mired in the same fear as the other teams. They might not be preoccupied with manufactured num-bers. They might be a well-functioning group doing a superior job. In the end, this section may not have won the "friendly" competition, nor met a predetermined quota. Their output num-bers may look below average, but are probably statistically more accurate, because they aren't afraid to tell the true story.

A fiefdom structure ultimately smothers potential and can punish some of the most valuable, but unrecognized, members of the organization.

SERFS USUALLY STAY ON THE ESTATE

In larger companies, fiefdoms can exist more subtly—mirroring the organizational structure of divisions or departments—but if the lines of communication are drawn like a box around the division, even if the communication inside the division is good, the results can be devastating to the company as a whole.

Let me give an example:

In this instance, I had traveled out of town to work with a client. When I arrived at the airport, I was picked up by one of the employees in a company car. I was given gourmet coffee and welcomed to the town. I was impressed. The employee's task that day was handling our schedule and telling me about the company. I was told the ride to the business would take about thirty minutes. My attention was drawn to the vehicle we would be using. It was a well-publicized SUV model in which I had never ridden. The fit and finish appeared quite good and the attention to detail appeared to be above average. I liked the looks of it and was eager for the ride to begin. I was visiting a quality company and I was sure they wanted to be associated with, and use, quality vehicles.

The thirty-minute drive was an education. It being the summer months, we used the air conditioner. Even at low level, the noise it generated made talking a challenge, so the conversation was fragmented at best. In addition, the passenger front seat offered little lumbar support and when slid fully aft still subjected me to a "formal" ride with my knees gently nudging the dash.

The vehicle was meant to please a broad spectrum of the

market. As a result, the suspension was designed to address many needs while accomplishing none of them. We were subjected to every crack in the road and change of highway condition. Upon arrival, I had a stiff back and a highway experience that was marginal, if not below standard. By the way, we sure looked good getting to our destination.

My point is, all the parts of the vehicle were quality. The fit and finish were to a high level, but the components had clearly been developed and organized separately. Put together, all of those excellent pieces made for a very uncomfortable ride. Isn't it the same in many of our organizations? We might have a passion for quality and invest heavily in research and design, but we become so obsessed with the individual parts, divisions and sections that we forget what the customer needed in the first place.

Management expected the parts of that car to fit together, but committed the gravest of errors; they assumed success. Faithful employees worked hard, were dedicated to their job, wanted good results, and built individual components that produced a failed product. Engineering didn't talk to Design or share information. Design didn't communicate with Production and Customer Research. The product had rolled off the assembly line gleaming and polished and I couldn't wait to roll out of it!

How often do we find that different work units of an organization operating with the best of intentions are actually in conflict with each other? Supervisors are supposedly competent in their own fields, yet they are unaware of the problems other managers may be experiencing. Is work duplicated in your organization? Does information you need already exist in another fiefdom, but you don't know it? Have you ever considered how much money is wasted in corporate America when two fiefdoms develop the same information and fail to communicate?

And so, a corporate fiefdom can be created through internal competition and power-grabbing or, perhaps more innocently, it can be a result of strict adherence to an arbitrary organizational chart. In either case, if information isn't flowing throughout the organization, you've got fiefdoms. And they need some scrutiny.

TO MARKET, TO MARKET

Where does the customer fit into the corporate fiefdom? Unfortunately, the answer is often, "Not at all." Chances are, that if management is too busy playing the "My Estate is the Best, Gold Star Award" game, they are not listening within the company, nor are they listening to the customer. And here is the key:

The Way To Beat the Corporate Fiefdom System Is To Always Keep Your Eye on the Customer.

Regardless of your product or service, if you've created an atmosphere of true concern that constantly asks what the customer wants or needs, the fiefdoms can't survive. Concern for the customer means asking questions, inside and outside the organization. Asking questions requires listening for the answers. If someone is open to information from anywhere, then information is free to flow, fiefdom barriers dissolve and the chances of missing the mark in the marketplace are greatly reduced.

LORDS A-LEAPIN'

In the Middle Ages, serfs were forced to declare loyalty to their feudal lords. In corporate fiefdoms, the lords are no different (although technically, we should be calling some of them ladies.) While one can find many excellent managers in these fragmented organizations, the structure supports and encourages destructive management styles. The IDYL (I Demand Your Loyalty) and MDOF (My Door Is Open To Favorites) management styles reign supreme. For some managers, someone is a team player if he or she doesn't criticize the boss or one of the boss's decisions. These managers not only create the fiefdoms, but reinforce the system. They build their empires at the cost of employee well-being, customer satisfaction and, inevitably, the company's ability to reach its full potential.

How do we recognize a fiefdom? Is there a way to catch a fiefdom-in-progress without waiting for a crisis? Certainly. There are many ways, which most concerned leaders—once aware of the problem—will fix on intuitively. One quick check, however, is to simply attend a meeting.

Because we are bringing a group of people together, we tend to assume that the purpose of a meeting is communication. In a corporate fiefdom, a meeting is often about power.

Watch.

- Is the focus of the meeting to review or assign quotas or objectives? Are some groups being rewarded while others are left to feel somehow inadequate? Is this creating a team environment or a fiefdom?

- Is information withheld or used for power or status? In fiefdoms, information is a weapon. It does not flow freely.

- Is there a free exchange of ideas or are many of the people who are attending keeping their mouths shut? Lords do not like to be contradicted.

- Is management assigning tasks to teams or other individuals that really should be theirs? A sure way to keep the lord at the head of the fiefdom is to defer high-risk decisions or tasks to the serfs. Then, later, if heads roll, the blame is easily shifted. At the same time, the lord always has the option to override the team (that can feel good) or at least take the credit for success.

- Is the meeting a combination of serfs and lords? If it feels that way, then it is. If there's no fiefdom, there is nobody at the meeting to whom you could apply those labels.

While meeting culture is a quick indicator of whether a fiefdom exists in your organization, another important measure is fear. Are employees afraid of their boss? Are they afraid to make a decision or voice an opinion? Are they smiling or frowning? Certainly, any one individual can be fearful at work, but what we're looking for here is a prevailing atmosphere of fear. Are people supportive and enthusiastic about projects outside their own domains, or are they secretive and jealous of success? No one individual can provide an accurate measure, but by asking questions and really listening, it is possible to take the temperature of a group and learn a great deal about how a portion of the corporate society is functioning.

If you find a problem, fix it. Fiefdoms kill the human spirit and individual potential. Success takes leadership, from the top down. And, it takes understanding what really makes employees, and thus your business, thrive. Sometimes, as you'll see, the employees themselves don't even know what that really is.

WHAT ABOUT THOSE SERFS?

The American Heritage Dictionary describes fiefdom as, "the estate or domain of a feudal lord. Something over which one dominant person or group exercises control." Alone, that definition might not be too scary, but ask yourself: "In a fiefdom, what happens to the serfs?"

Collective bargaining units were formed because management goofed. This statement is not in support of collective bargaining. I have seen examples where the collective bargaining unit became the employees' worst enemy. In one company I worked with, it became even more myopic than the organization whose workforce they were representing.

I have nothing against an organized workforce, and I won't address whether collective bargaining is relevant or not. One could write volumes on the principle of collective bargaining and its impact on the 20th century. You would have many opinions from a selection of viewpoints. One point is clear: Collective bargaining is a part of the universal workforce and will be for the foreseeable future. Its impact will vary with time, but it will remain a factor in employer/employee relations.

My hope, however, is that both management and the collective bargaining units figure out what's really important to the workforce instead of wasting so much time on issues that don't matter to employees in the long run. Let me explain.

There are several people who have studied what motivates people in the workplace. One of the most famous of these researchers is Frederick Herzberg who developed what he calls Hygiene Theory and Motivation Theory. Hygiene Theory involves aspects of the workplace such as salary, status, and working conditions. The Motivation Theory focuses on the job itself and how achievement and recognition, for example, affect motivation.

I choose to look at motivators in a slightly different way and refer to them as Short-Term and Long-Term Motivators.

SHORT-TERM MOTIVATORS:

Advancement: Gaining a promotion or step up in a job is a short-term issue. If you get a promotion, or are one of several candidates, the anticipation is considerable. You picture yourself in the position and visualize how wonderful your world will be if you get the promotion. So the promotion does occur. How long until the novelty wears off? The most would be thirty, sixty or maybe ninety days. Then what?

New Policies: Let's say management introduces a new policy that will give an extra eight hours each year as a personal day off. It's rolled out by the executive staff and introduced as a greater step in the company communication policy. Now, maybe management is giving it because they cannot afford the dollars for salary increases and this is the next best thing. It sounds good and it will be nice to plan an extra day off for your vacation this year. How long do you think the excitement lasts for the extra day off? The motivation stops as soon as the day is taken. Once it is gone, it is no longer a motivator. You now must wait one year to get excited about that benefit again. It is a great idea, but it's not lasting.

Salary: We all want to get paid a fair wage. We want to know that our bills are paid and we have money for emergencies, but we must also recognize that money is not a long-term motivator. Money does motivate, but not long term. Again, if you get a promotion or wage increase or some other type of merit pay, how long does the excitement last? Most salary increases are spent either psychologically or physically before the first increase hits an employee's checking account. Once it is added into the household budget, what happens? How long does the newness of the extra money last? Remember, the majority of workers are in debt in direct proportion to the money they make. Oh, and by the way, if your boss doubled your salary tomorrow, would you now work twice as hard? The fixation on the dollar alone is a setup for long-term expectations from a short-term motivator.

Granted, many sales organizations rely on money as the motivator and even set up special money incentives to make specific products move. While I doubt that this system will change in the near future, I think we should ask ourselves who is really served by this arrangement. Obviously, the salespeople like it because they make good money. Shouldn't they make good money, anyway? Theirs is a tough job. Often, in this money-directed environment, the reward is not necessarily tied directly to the effort. One salesperson might have an easier, therefore more lucrative, territory. Another might have a fantastic assistant who services the customers so efficiently and pleasantly that the repeat sales rate is exceptionally high. In that case, shouldn't the assistant be getting the bonuses and trips to Hawaii? I also question the motive of moving a particular product. While in the short-term, the company wins, is that a positive long-term approach? What if the sales force's excellent sales technique is selling a product the customers don't really need or want? Won't that hurt repeat sales down the line?

The other factor that must be addressed is that there is a small number of people who really are motivated by money. This is different than the response most of us have: We like it and we want more. For these people, their self-worth is measured in dollars and cents. These are the folks who are most hung up on status symbols and whose conversations are centered around what they bought last and how much everything costs. I concede that for these people, you can extract a big commitment in exchange for big bucks, but it seems a rather spiritless, empty exchange for establishing employee reward systems, doesn't it? And, for most people, it simply will not work long term.

Work Conditions: This one is a real sleeper. Wouldn't you be thrilled if your computer was acting up and the boss said to you, "Tomorrow a brand new computer with giant hi-resolution flat screen forty-thousand color monitor, THX surround sound with the turbo-blowtorch processor is going to be placed on your desk." What an event! You've asked for months and here it is. When the computer arrives, you put it through all its paces for weeks and it is amazing...for a while. Everyone comes to your desk to see the newest machine in town and you just love the attention. What happens when the newness wears off or the person next to you gets a new computer and it has eighty-thousand colors on its monitor? Your excitement usually lasts until the next model comes out.

Much of working conditions are what you make of them. Yes, employers are required to provide a safe, harassment-free, work environment. But the attitude to do the job is the responsibility of the employee. That street runs one way.

LONG TERM MOTIVATORS:

Achievement: This factor gives employees the self-satisfaction of knowing they have set a goal, or in the case of a team project, a group goal, and they have reached the conclusion. The satisfaction is internal. What has happened is a transformation. When a sense of achievement is realized, it cannot be taken away. It becomes part of the employee's belief system.

Recognition: We all want to be recognized for what we have done and what we can do. This is not the gold star group party or where the office favorites get the usual smiles. Recognition is as simple as a supervisor walking up to an employee, and in a one-on-one situation, saying, "I like your work. You are an asset to the company. Keep it up." It is as simple as telling people they are valued and that what they do means something.

The Work Itself: I often pay attention when I hear someone say, "I love what I'm doing." I think these people have really found their niche and have a true sense of peace. Many work at what they do simply because they love it. It addresses their value system and they find that the principal motivator.

I worked with a client who made custom wood furnishings. One woman on the assembly line, whose job was to sand cabinet doors for eight hours a day, had been with the organization for close to twenty years. She loved her job. Her work showed it, too. This woman knew her job and understood how it related to the entire piece of furniture that was being made. Her pride was obvious. As a side note, I wouldn't want to get in her way, either! Her work area ran like a Swiss watch. Money was important, but more was involved. She worked for an organization that focused on all employees and how they relate to the company. The front line was trained, educated and knew how what they did contributed to the greater good.

Responsibility: Probably one of the greatest compliments you can give an employee is to give him or her more responsibility. Giving responsibility is telling an employee that you trust them and value their decisions, work habits, dedication, and that you value them as people. The foundation of responsibility is trust. Working people must have trust to survive.

You can increase responsibility for almost any employee if you educate, empower and raise the standard of expectation. Most people will rise to the level of the expectation and seek greater levels of productivity. There are some people who do not want the added responsibility, but in that case, there are other issues involved.

Let's go back for a moment to the collective bargaining issues and their relation to management. The first four issues I mentioned, Advancement, New Policies, Salary, and Work Conditions, are all short-term motivators. While temporarily satisfying, they do not add to the psychological growth of the employee.

Now, think for a minute, where do we often see these short-term motivators come up? If you have ever been involved in collective bargaining you know that the main issues that are bargained for with most labor contracts are the short-term motivators, not the long-term ones. Let's take a moment and think about this dynamic.

During the bargaining process, both sides put their respective issues on the table. They negotiate, mediate, and hopefully reach an agreement. If they do not, outside parties are brought in to further mediate the process. During this time, employees become polarized over the lack of progress, management digs in its heels and the employees and collective bargaining unit dig in a little deeper. If an agreement still can't be reached, then you go to fact finding. This process can take months. If the process now becomes too hostile, the only answer may be binding arbitration. This can be bad for both sides because a third party will make the decision both sides have to live with.

But what do we really have here? All the time this is going on the employees are watching the process take—what looks like—forever. Frustration and anger grow to the point where serious morale issues can develop. As the frustration issues continue to grow, a settlement is reached and, for the sake of simplicity here, labor gets what it asked for. Employees chant that they won, yet the finger pointing and alienation continues.

If I'm correct in my assessment of short-term issues, then labor, who got the numbers they wanted, really lost the most. What did the settlement really achieve? You now have a company where you have frustrated and angry employees making more money under better external working conditions.

Addressing the short-term factors only addresses the symptoms of the problem. Did the agreement address the betterment of the corporate culture? Did the agreement enhance the working environment for all employees? Did the agreement further strengthen the trust between labor and management? And the most important question, will this agreement mean a higher quality product will roll off the assembly line and be bought by a happier customer?

I would suggest that the short-term factors are the issues taken to the table because they are the easiest to quantify. We can negotiate percentage raises, time off, and so forth, but my guess is that what most employees are really upset about when they square off with management are the intangibles, the long-term motivators. Or, to use my vocabulary, they are missing nourishment for their spirit.

I want to digress for a moment and look at another aspect of labor/management conflict. When an organization is fighting against itself, the question needs to be asked, "Who is minding the store?" When management's focus is pulled from directing and running the company and the front-line employees are un-motivated and angry, it's a setup for catastrophe.

An interesting phenomenon occurred in the commercial aviation industry that illustrates my point. The National Trans-portation Safety Board has recorded instances where the flight crew flew commercial airliners into the ground. What happened was the aircraft experienced an in-flight mechanical problem that required the cockpit crew to handle the emergency. As the crew started to address and even solve the problem, both pilots be-came so engrossed in the matters at hand that they drew their focus away from the most important task—flying the airplane. The initial emergency was not of the nature where it would have resulted in a loss of life or major injuries, but the crew became so focused on the short-term issues that they did nothing more than take a perfectly good airplane right to the scene of the accident.

My point is both an observation and a note of caution. La-bor and management can become transfixed on short-term prob-lems and pull their attention away from the real point at hand: "flying the company." Their lack of attention can let the com-pany proceed toward a much larger corporate disaster than any-one imagined. When that happens, both labor and management lose. In a time of crisis or diversion in the company, find out who is "flying the airplane." They must continue to lead the company at all costs and it would seem that labor would want them to do so. Their future might depend on it.

Management is responsible for what happens to everyone. It is responsible and accountable for the system and operation. It is responsible for letting corporate fiefdoms flourish in the organization.

Any type of corporate fiefdom is a diversion from productivity. Corporate fiefdoms can doom a product, a process, and productivity. In fiefdoms, people forget what real team participation means. They duplicate work or costs and keep information from other parts of the company. They develop a spirit of antagonism instead of a spirit of cooperation and pride. The view of the customer is obscured completely and employees focus on, and may even fight for, what they want, but not what they need.

What needs to change? Leadership. The company leaders set the tone, the ethic, and the spiritual essence of the company. If the leaders change their perspective, the rest of the company will follow.

In the twenty-first century, I would like to see each organization look upon itself as:

- a skills-based enterprise meeting the needs of its customers.
- looking out for the well being of an adaptive workforce.

- promoting an environment where employees work without fear and enjoy their work.
- addressing long-term motivators and not just short-term factors.
- a magnet for new ideas and methods.
- developing and listening to the voices of both management and the front-line employees.

Is your company making individual quality pieces, but none of them seem to "fit" together for a final product? Is customer satisfaction the focus of every employee at every level? Managers today need to be listening and teaching new principles and ways of managing and communicating. Otherwise, they may eventually fall victim to the very fiefdoms they have created.

It takes courage and dedication to be a leader instead of a lord.

Long live the leaders.

MANY MANAGERS MEASURE EMPLOYEE PRODUCTIVITY

AND SET OBJECTIVES WITH PERCENTILES AND

COMPARTMENTALIZED JOB DESCRIPTIONS.

THE HUMAN SPIRIT, WHICH IS THE BASIS FOR

PRODUCTIVITY, DOES NOT RESPOND IN PERCENTILES

AND PREDEFINED OUTCOMES.

Forms, Functions, and Failures of the American Workplace

"Eighty percent of American managers cannot answer with any measure of confidence these seemingly simple questions: What is my job? What in it really counts? How well am I doing?"

W. Edwards Deming
Management Consultant and Author

Organizational Charts

The management legacy Industrial America has left us has outlived its usefulness. It is the linear, rigid style of management that revolves around scheduling, autocratic supervision, organizational charts and job descriptions. This is not to say that structure is unimportant. It is merely to suggest that in some ways our existing structures do not make sense and that perhaps it's time to seek new ways.

Empowerment is a big buzzword in management circles, but

do we really think about what the word "empower" means? Here are a few synonyms: grant, sanction, enable, decontrol, and liberate. These sound great, don't they? But how can empowerment work in an environment that is defined by the terms department, division, section, unit, and classification?

Let's look at some definitions for these organizational words:

Department: "to separate and divide, a specialty."

Division: "a boundary or partition that serves to divide or keep separate."

Section: "to cut or to separate and divide into parts."

Classification: "systematic grouping into categories."

I think we're sending mixed messages. How do we decontrol and liberate while at the same time we divide and create partitions? If we want empowered employees, does that mean we empower throughout the organization or only by section, division, or unit?

Linear organizations can be comfortable environments. Everyone knows what is expected. Everything is defined. But linear organizations have trouble supporting creativity, and if both the organizational chart and the job descriptions are rigid enough, important information and functions will inevitably fall through the cracks. Not only that, but the divisions could even be causing counterproductive intracompany competition. The beauty of this system is, of course, that nobody has to take responsibility for anything as long as his or her own little box on the chart is functioning according to plan. This is "cover your bases" company thinking.

In her book, *Leadership and the New Science: Learning About Organization From an Orderly Universe*, Margaret Wheatley contends that if given time, a group of people will self-organize in ways that do not require traditional management and the structures it represents. If left alone, employees will create a language and communication style around new ideas and information they receive. Because they arrive at new ways of doing things through self-discovery, they have ownership in their jobs. Employees who are actively invested in their work rarely utter the words, "I can't do that. It's not in my job description."

This is not to suggest that we tear down all the structures we have and invite anarchy into our businesses until the new structures self-organize. Most of us don't have time for that, but it is important to recognize this ability in humans and to stay open to opportunities that allow the self-organizing mechanism to flourish.

For example, a manager might supervise a number of teams. He or she might want to keep the teams intact, but instead of all the teams having the same structure, each of the teams could divide the work according to the talents and interests of the members. The tasks might be more fluid and cooperative in some groups than in others.

Here's a simple illustration. Most of us have eaten in busy

restaurants where we constantly have to flag down our server for more water or another drop of coffee. We can see that the server is covering several tables. A second server, who is assigned a different group of tables, walks by with a pitcher of water. Does he or she stop or go on by?

Sometimes if you watch a pair of servers, you'll notice that they are working cooperatively, picking up empty plates for each other as they go by, or filling coffee cups all around if they have the pot in their hand. On another day, with a different pair of servers, it's clearly "my tables, your tables." Each is more comfortable doing his or her own work and not having to feel responsible for anything apart from that.

The restaurant management might have a policy about how these teams are required to work. The danger is in being too heavy-handed and controlling for the task at hand, and not recognizing the personal dynamics of the employees involved. If the manager decides that each server must stick to his or her own tables, there are times when one server gets too busy and half of the customers might not get good service. If the manager insists on cooperative work under all circumstances, the less motivated server will get away with shifting the load to the other server and there will be hard feelings. Half the customers get marginal service, and the other half get a harried, grumpy server. By giving employees space to self-organize in appropriate situations, management is often allowing each team to find a way that works to everyone's benefit.

Be aware, however, that allowing self-organization does not equate with hands-off, let-'em-sink-or-swim management. Leadership takes energy and wisdom. The task for leadership is to know the appropriate settings for self-organization and to secure the outcome by creating and insisting upon a positive process.

JOB DESCRIPTIONS

I've come to wonder if job descriptions are a blessing or a curse. Job descriptions, or at least titles, can help customers navigate the labyrinth of a corporate structure and help employees know where their responsibilities end and another's begin. For some employees, it is important to know exactly what expectations are placed upon them. In other cases, where an employee tends to overestimate his or her abilities and importance, a job description prevents unpleasant conflict. Job descriptions can take the subjectivity out of daily operations. And so, as a catalog of corporate functions, job descriptions, in theory, increase efficiency and communication.

Unfortunately, I believe that our reliance on job descriptions has caused some undesirable side effects. They become excuses for all kinds of problems. Employees aren't kept in the information loop because their job descriptions don't specify that they need the information. Other employees get away with less effort because the job description doesn't specify any extra exertion. Important tasks fall through the cracks because they weren't specifically anticipated and included in anybody's job description.

Collective bargaining's focus on job descriptions comes from a defensive posture. Job descriptions insure the employees don't have to do anything extra for which they won't get paid. While this is important, and I recognize that there have been abuses historically, too often it translates into a worker attitude of being sure there's not "more giving than getting" at any time.

Certainly, workers have a right to seek protection from inequitable situations, but job descriptions place people in boxes and treat them as cogs in a wheel. When labor negotiators insist on rigid job descriptions, they need to ask themselves what happens to the heart and soul of the workers they are trying to protect.

Employers use job descriptions in other equally defensive ways. Job descriptions keep them out of court. Also, job descriptions provide a measure of control to those managers who are afraid to lead. If you want to control an employee, control his or her environment. A job description does just that. It tells employees what they may do and, effectively, what they may not do. It tells them, "Do your job and get your salary. We don't expect anything more from you, so don't expect more from us."

The boxes we draw around employees' responsibilities also draw boxes around people's thoughts, feelings, and creativity. Often employees are hired, become excited about their jobs, see opportunity for growth and embark on a steep learning curve that challenges them and rewards them spiritually. Then, within a few short years, those same employees, who had once been so eager, are confronted with a new task or some other change and the response has become, "That's not in my job description." Something in the organization has made the box created by the job description the only safe place in the company, one that must be defended.

I can hear some managers crying out already, "The problem is with the employees. They have a bad attitude."

Let me tell you a story.

A few years ago, I was providing training for a public service organization. During one of the sessions, we discussed career burnout, upward versus lateral mobility, and the unwritten barriers that often exist in organizations. After class, one of the students approached me and related his recent experience in the organization.

He enjoyed his work and wanted to expand his education and job tasks and had therefore approached his supervisor and asked for some additions to his job description. He realized that because of the way the organization was structured, the additions would result in a small pay raise, but more importantly, it would enable him to become involved in different areas of the company. The supervisor instructed him to write up a proposal and submit it to Human Resources. He did. Two weeks later he had his response. It was in the form of a memo. The employee would not be reclassified because they already had the allotted number of people at the next salary step. They would not rewrite his job description and he was to remain at his present classification and pay scale.

Here is the interesting part. In the memo, the Human Resources Manager stated the following: "Position classification does not recognize work quality, nor comparison responsibilities with co-workers; but rather it is simple categorizing of position descriptions into pigeonholes called classifications. The question to be addressed is…'is your position description more closely related to one of two classifications…'"

Here was an employee who was looking for meaning in his daily work. The personnel department told him that the company could not let him improve organizationally or intellectually because the pigeonhole he wanted to move into was already full. His drive was not applauded or even recognized, and he received no encouragement that a slot might ever open up.

This young man was ready to contribute more to the company. He was ready to invest and serve, but he was more motivated than the company wanted him to be. The message to him was plain. "We have no room here for inspired workers. Please go back to being a cog in the wheel and don't bother us further." He didn't. He left.

Is this how we "manage" our human resources? If our own employees are nothing more than slips of paper to be processed and classified, is it any wonder that our customers are not getting the attention they deserve?

We have inherited some long-standing habits and have reaped the benefit of them in the workplace. "It's not in my job description" must be one of the costliest phrases in the American workplace, yet our organizational structures perpetuate and encourage just that attitude.

It is costly and difficult to change old habits. It is devastating not to.

PERFORMANCE OBJECTIVES

Set the goals and analyze the results. It sounds logical doesn't it? It's scientific. Smart business, right? Certainly, stockholders want to see those numbers working away, and it is important to quantify information in ways people can understand. Still, the numbers game is dangerous, especially when you use numbers to measure people.

We have succumbed to the idea that numbers are knowledge. They aren't. Some numbers aren't even information. I have seen astonishing numbers cited and established as goals. They are beautiful, exciting numbers. They have nothing to do with reality or with the big picture. They are simply feel-good objectives that made some manager in some meeting look good. Despite a manager's best intentions at the outset, goals are often politically driven, not customer driven, and they are established with little regard to the costs in human terms or in the dollars they will cost. Worse yet, the benefits of achieving them are not even necessarily clear.

But even if we set aside this jaded perspective, it's important to question where some of these numbers originate and why. Many managers are not given the training to properly understand the implications of the data for which they are responsible. They develop tunnel vision and focus on setting objectives that are independent of the rest of the organization. Or, they respond to objectives provided by another department whose numbers might have been derived in a flawed fashion. The result can be as disjointed as if the violins in a symphony orchestra interpreted a work as a romantic ballad and the cellos thought it was a funeral dirge. If there isn't a conductor to set the tone, or if the groups don't communicate, you get cacophony.

Let's look at an example. Let's say the crime rate in a town spikes up and the powers that be set a goal to reduce burglaries by 10%. Sounds great, doesn't it? How do we go about doing this? The obvious answer is to hire more officers, teach the citizens how to prevent burglaries, and encourage citizen involvement in reporting potential burglaries in progress.

The problem with this scenario is that while everyone likes the idea of burglaries being reduced by 10%, the establishment of the goal and the decisions about how to go about meeting it didn't take into account the existing system or how it would be affected. It could be that something in the existing system would make it difficult for the new officers to be effective. It could be that there are already plenty of officers and that the problem is in dispatch failing to ask the right questions and apply the right code to crimes in progress. It could be that the paperwork has increased for the existing officers to the extent that they have become inefficient and that the addition of new officers would have only a marginal effect, while examination and adjustment of the paper flow might have a dramatic effect in freeing up officer time. It might even be that the actual incidence of crime hasn't risen. It could be that thanks to increased citizen involvement (an element restated as part of the new goal) more crimes are being reported than before, or that the way the crime statistics are compiled has changed.

What's missing so often as we set goals and quotas is that we fail to look at the entire system. We need to look at the interaction of all the elements involved. Any time we roll out a number-based statement that feels like "reduce burglaries by 10%" we ought to recognize it as a red flag. We need to find out where that number came from. If it's a feel-good "about right" number, we know immediately that the system wasn't considered in the generation of that number.

This process of using numbers to analyze and work within the interactions of a system—statistical process tools —is a powerful way to quantify what's happening in an organization and to establish new goals. It is the opposite of the mentality that maximizes the parts to maximize the whole. It looks at the whole to begin with. Statistical process tools enable the system to generate meaningful numbers that enable us to produce a better system. This is so much more productive than trying to produce better numbers.

Let's look at the effect of setting arbitrary performance objectives without looking at the entire system. In an autocratic system, managers set arbitrary quotas and time frames. The goal is to motivate the front-line workers, but the workers, because they are smart, realize that if they meet the goals easily, the next goals will be harder to reach. Any suggestions the employees might have to improve the system are left unspoken because they have no confidence that the effect of any changes to the system won't be negative for them personally. As a result, the cost of the product is too high and the opportunity for increased efficiency is lost.

Sometimes, management recognizes this problem and takes steps to address it by asking the employees to study a problem and suggest a solution. The employees are not empowered to implement or test their ideas and they have to rely on management giving a thumbs up or a thumbs down to whatever they suggest. If management happens to veto the suggestions, the employees feel that they were put through a useless exercise that management thought would boost morale. The employees are insulted and feel that their time and energy were wasted.

Other companies are unwilling to look at the system at all because they use past behavior to make future projections. If they shake up the system, they lose control of the outcomes. Even if those outcomes might be better than the present ones, the uncertainty of their numbers makes change too risky. These companies remind me of someone trying to drive the car by looking only in the rear view mirror. "We can tell where we're going by where we've been." Not a lot of vision there.

The worst scenario is when the organization distorts the data to make the system look better without really analyzing the system or the effect of the reactions to the data. A perfect example is when schools systematically pass students to the next grade level, without provisions for special help, before the students are ready to do the work for that grade level. The class test averages change, and because the teachers recognize the different ability levels, the expectations are altered and the curriculum is modified so the lower scoring students aren't left behind. Ironically, the school looks better, because a higher percentage of students are being advanced, but the education level is the same, or even suffers, because teachers have to teach to a broader range of student skill levels.

Then another number comes in. The benchmark tests. If the school isn't doing well on the benchmark tests, the community is unhappy. Therefore, the teacher must focus on teaching to the test in order to keep the numbers up. The more pressure there is for the students to produce good numbers on the measuring stick, the more class time is spent on preparing students for the tests. The test scores are no longer a measuring tool to provide information to the teachers, they have become the end result. The role of the teachers has changed from educating and motivating students to producing higher test scores. Increasing the benchmarks doesn't necessarily mean a better product (i.e., better educated students) it just forces the school to do a better job generating the numbers.

If an employee is told that his or her job or compensation depends upon meeting a quota, then the employee will make the numbers work. What else can the employee do? Management will be given numbers it wants to hear, one way or the other. The criteria for evaluation and inspection will be changed to fit the scenario. Arbitrary figures will be created without analysis and used to set new goals. *"If we gained 6% this month then why can't we do 7% next month?"* I want to know where the 7% came from and how the new goal will affect the system. Is that 1% increase the best use of resources? Will it have an effect on the end product? What will it cost the front-line employees and the company to achieve it?

The front line has learned that if management is happy then day-to-day life improves dramatically. The short-term goal might be met, but the result is that the product becomes numbers and not a quality product. The managers get what they asked for, but did they get what they really wanted? Going back to the example of the teachers, they've achieved the good test scores that were demanded of them, but they probably don't have inspired students.

Performance objectives, as we've traditionally applied them, create a downward spiral. Employees who are caught in the numbers game eventually realize that even if they don't know the cause, the meaning has gone out of their work life. Good numbers don't resonate in the heart and soul of the employee, so unless the numbers are being generated with the goal of an improved process and the clear mission of the organization in sight, productivity will ultimately suffer. The best workers will leave, and morale will sink. Management will respond by trying to motivate the remaining employees with new numbers. Eventually, the numbers, too, will go down the drain. Management will look for the problem everywhere but in the objective-setting process. Everyone will see the failure to meet the objectives as the symptom of the problem, but will never stop to think that the objectives themselves contributed to the problem.

Management continues to forget that the front-line employee is a rapid learner. Word gets around. Workers know if policies have become short-sighted or off-base. Front-line employees can smell the loss of integrity a mile away and they respond to it. They have been there before, faced with predetermined outcomes that were flawed before they ever hit the front line. They've been held accountable for meaningless goals and measurement strategies that undermine productivity. They've been faced with performance objectives that could better have been established by throwing a dart at a dartboard. With the challenges of responding to the productivity game, is it any wonder employees lose sight of the customer and hide behind their job descriptions? The job description becomes the only safe haven against management craziness.

Let me illustrate this concept further. A government agency I know of set a long list of performance measures. Each objective had a separate percentile or goal for the employees to reach. Management set the goals. After about a year, it became evident, even to the managers, that there were too many separate measures. The employees were up in arms and only a few of the goals were being met.

The managers got together and decided to eliminate more than half of the objectives. This pleased the employees, but then the managers decided that with half of the *objectives* gone, the employees must now have extra time on their hands, so they raised the expectations for the remaining goals. In their view, they were practicing good management. They responded to the employees, they set new goals, and now they could expect success. They were so blinded by the process that they failed to consider the problems with the objectives in the first place and to consider if their expectations were even reasonable. They failed to consider the impact of the new expectations or the desirability of having them met. They didn't consider whether the goals were realistic, but they were good-sounding goals. Nothing showed management that the bar needed to be raised. It was simply done. They certainly couldn't let the employees get away with having less expected of them, and the benefit to the customers was left out of the equation altogether.

But here's the beauty of the performance measure dance for this set of managers. Having "responded to the employees and adjusted the targets," the responsibility for the failure of the program now rested on the employees' shoulders, not on theirs. What might appear as the best of intentions may actually be setting up the front-line employees for failure.

The Other Half of the Story—Performance Appraisals

Goals, on their own, are needed. They can be motivating, and if employees are given objectives in the spirit of knowledge management, goals can be an integral part of an efficient and productive organization. So the problem isn't with goals, per se, as long as they are goals based on value, knowledge and an understanding of people and not politics. The problem can be with the big stick at the other end of the process called the performance appraisal.

In many companies, performance and financial compensation are directly linked to the rankings an employee achieves on the often poorly conceived performance objectives we've just discussed. The employee's worth to the company is distilled into percentiles and quotas. This is especially true in manufacturing environments. Less tangible contributions that might have great value to the organization are discounted. The process becomes highly subjective and dehumanizing, and the employees often respond with feelings of powerlessness.

I heard an interview on the radio with a young man who had worked for a large national company. I might get the details wrong, but here is the essence of what he related. The interviewer asked how he got started in the organization.

"I was in customer service," he replied.

"You must have been great in that department," the interviewer replied.

"No, I was awful. It was a disaster ."

"I don't understand," answered the interviewer. "You're personable, dedicated, smart. What didn't work?"

"Well," the young man replied, "my first month there I thought I was doing a great job. I helped all these people, worked long hours. I thought I must be one of the best employees there. But then, at the end of the month, I got my ranking from the supervisor. I was 65th out of 120! I couldn't believe it. I was in the bottom half of the support people there."

"So what did you do?" the interviewer asked.

"I asked what the rankings were based on, and I was told it was the number of customers I helped. That was easy to fix. I started cutting off conversations mid-sentence very early in the call. I knew the customer would think something had happened to the call and would call back, and meantime, my phone statistics were stellar."

"Didn't you feel bad about that?" the interviewer asked.

"Well, a little, but I had to bring my ranking up. I wasn't about to sit there in the bottom half of the group."

Eventually, the young man left customer service. He moved up. He acknowledged in the interview that it began to bother him that he was getting recognition as an effective customer service representative when he knew he really wasn't doing a good job for the customer.

While not all employees will resort to drastic measures to improve their rankings, it can't be surprising when they do. Their future might depend on the numbers they generate.

Evaluation by rank on a performance objective might sound ideal to the managers who don't want to deal with the messy dynamics of human nature, but it isn't a fruitful attitude. If the people who are handing out the judgments have eliminated the human characteristics of cooperation, leadership, motivation, and effort, even the highest scoring participants will leave their appraisal meetings devalued and bitter.

If managers spent time measuring the effect of this objective/measurement game on employee productivity instead of wetting their fingers and sticking them in the air to determine new performance measures, I think they'd be surprised. I think they'd see clearly what happens when you base people's pay on numerical rankings and then tell them to go out to the floor and "be a team." I think they'd see how unfair it is to distribute a bonus based on performance measures one time and then when others meet the same objectives have no bonus available for them.

Sometimes, even without strict rankings, the rigidity of some performance appraisals is counterproductive. Years ago, I was called into my supervisor's office and told that we were reorganizing and that I was going to have field personnel assigned to me as well as the front-line employees I already supervised. I knew nothing about the duties of the field personnel and the written performance appraisals were due in one month.

Here is an excellent example of how we get so caught up in a system that we lose sight of the purpose we are trying to fulfill. I had little information about these employees. I had no way to evaluate how they had done their jobs during the past eleven months, what their individual strengths and challenges might be, or even what skills they needed to do their jobs well. Yet, the company insisted that the evaluations occur on schedule.

To me, the exercise was worthless to the company, except from the standpoint of cover-your-butt management—the reviews were in the files so we had fulfilled our obligation. It was unfair to the employees even though I modified the format of the review to make it more of an exchange of information than an evaluation. Because maintaining the organizational structure of the company was more important than the integrity of the employer/supervisor relationship, these employees lost the opportunity to get fruitful feedback and the opportunity for additional compensation or responsibilities in that period.

No one will argue that some type of appraisal system is necessary. Managers will always be subjective, and I recognize that the performance measure is a weak attempt to democratize the evaluation process. I would, however, argue that the present double-hit system of performance objective/appraisal is not only obsolete, it is harmful, and the same goes for some of the newer incarnations of the concept. "Pay for performance" is one of the most disastrous programs ever devised. Money is not a long-term motivator. If managers sitting behind their desks feel they have solved the motivation problem by dangling a dollar bill on a stick, they are missing the point. If the workplace does not nurture the human spirit, no amount of money will matter over time.

It also doesn't work to have the employees set their own measures. Now the employees are evaluated not only on how well they met the measures, but how well they set them. If they set ambitious goals and meet them, what will they do to please the evaluator next period? Set higher goals? When a plane reaches cruising altitude, is it really necessary to make it go higher? Where employees and productivity are concerned, there is the inevitable expectation. More. Better. It's like telling the football team they made a first down, but we're moving the goal line out.

What Do We Do Instead?

We might need to formalize some aspects of management, but in doing so we must keep the human priorities in mind. Admiral Grace Hopper, United States Navy, Ret., said it best. "You cannot manage men into battle," she said. "You manage *things*; you *lead* people."

To me, the solutions to the problems we work so hard to quantify in terms of organizational charts, job descriptions, and the performance measure/appraisal game, can all be found in the human equation. When we are children, we look to our parents for our basic needs and for encouragement, meaning, positive models and guidance so we can succeed in the world. We all know that most children thrive in an environment where those elements exist and most are motivated to work hard.

Are our needs as adults in the workplace really so different?

I have to wonder why companies have to set up an annual schedule to let employees know where they stand in the organization. It seems to me that if the managers were communicating and leading, the employees would know how they were doing at all times. What is happening in organizations that would lead employees to have doubts about what their status is at any time?

I know that some managers will protest that formal performance appraisals are motivators. If performance appraisals are designed to motivate, try this test. Ask your Human Resources Department for the best appraisal system they have. If it will work on employees, it should also be adaptable to the family arena. It should work on your spouse and children.

Take it home and try it! If you really want to motivate them, make a file for each member of the family and put a job description in it with lots of notes they know you are taking, but which they can't see. Then, set about ranking your children. It might be hard for the child who is ranked lowest in the performance evaluations, but if your ranking system is fair, it should only motivate that child to work harder, right? Which of your children would be above average and which below? If you rank your children, then one has to be last and one first, otherwise you have no system. If you don't have several children, maybe you want to compare them with the neighborhood children and give them approval and allowance based on how they measure up. Sit down with your spouse on a regular basis and specify areas where he or she might improve, too. Be sure to have lots of documentation.

I think you see my point. Obviously, using this type of system on your family would be catastrophic, yet that is what we do to people every day in the workplace. In what way does ranking employees serve the company, the customer, or the unique human spirit that is each employee? It might appear to make the paperwork better, but does that end justify the means?

Each employee, regardless of the pay scale or responsibility, is a unique human spirit possessing his or her own combination of God-given talents. Why do we insist on dehumanizing those whose special talents don't register on the performance evaluation radar? They might still be valuable members of the organization. The workplace is different than the family, but the needs of the people are the same.

Employees will produce something, whether it is positive or negative for the company, and even in the best environments, there must be managers. But I ask that we look at what managers could accomplish if they were not so preoccupied with objectives and numbers and structures and preserving the organizational management dogma. Look at what managers could become:

- Coaches and mentors instead of judges and juries.
- Communicators who aren't afraid of a knowledgeable workforce.
- Listeners who keep the interests of the employee and the customer in mind.
- Organizers who set up structures that complement the needs of the employee and customer while enhancing the company bottom line.

The challenge is before us. The traditional structures we've held onto, and have hidden behind for so long, are no longer serving the American workplace. We have the information we need to create a new model that replaces the old system—a system that produces mistrust and devaluation—with a new structure that puts recognition of the human spirit at the front. There are many companies and organizations already thriving under this approach. Yes, there will need to be organization and accountability and goal setting. I'm not suggesting that we throw out the business with the old structures. But the new structures must be based on employee growth, a common goal of customer satisfaction, a tireless management training and recruitment program and an appreciation for non-linear thinking. We must learn how to use statistical analysis to improve processes in a meaningful way instead of applying arbitrary and destructive performance objectives. We need to rethink the role of managers and management in the workplace. We must help them to actively lead our workplace into a more fulfilling, productive, self-organized and idea-rich environment.

WE CANNOT HEAR THE VOICE OF OUR EMPLOYEES

BECAUSE OF THE NOISE CREATED BY THE CONSTANT

REBUILDING OF THE ORGANIZATIONAL CHART.

THE HUMAN SPIRIT DOES NOT RESPOND TO NOR

UNDERSTAND WORDS SUCH AS DIVISION OR SECTION.

ACCOUNTABILITY AND EMPOWERMENT

"Only through adventurous thinking can the search for new knowledge succeed. Without this knowledge, the world would stagnate as a pool without an inlet; neither would there be an outlet for its progress."

David Sarnoff
Founder and President, RCA

We are confusing the terms accountability and empowerment. Somewhere the myth has arisen that if you hold someone accountable then you have somehow also empowered them to make necessary changes. So often in today's workplace, the accountability is there, but not the power.

This goes much beyond the situation where an employee gets a new title and new responsibilities, but no pay raise or authority. This kind of situation is all too common and any alert manager should be able to spot such scenarios and fix them. I am talking more about whether managers have provided the environment and tools that enable an employee to succeed. Do we evaluate whether or not an employee truly has ability, either as a person, or as an element of the organization, to perform a task?

Let's look at the components that go into real empowerment.

KNOWLEDGE VS. INFORMATION

To me, the distinction between knowledge and information is vast, and corporate America has simply become too lazy to recognize which they are feeding their employees.

Data is easy to handle. It is loyal to no one and can be accumulated and massaged and broadcast to the world. Companies love to distribute data because it's easy—and therefore relatively cheap—to do so. But that is only half the process. Data by itself requires that the person receiving the information analyze it and draw conclusions.

That's where knowledge comes in. To respond productively to new information, one must have enough experience and knowledge of the larger implications to filter the data and find meaningful applications for it. Humans are good at this. We love to figure out how new information might change our view of an activity, a goal, a policy, a company, or even the world. And, as we know, a change of view often requires a change of action. That can be threatening.

Information comes from data crunching. It can be controlled. Knowledge, on the other hand is slippery, and charts its own course within each human as information forms and reshapes itself according to the unique perspective of the individual. Knowledge is the wonderful dynamic that makes humans so special, that enables us to accomplish great things, but it is unpredictable and impossible to manage.

And so, managers are left with a quandary. They need to empower their employees, but exactly how does that happen? Frankly, some managers find knowledgeable employees frightening. They withhold both information and education out of personal weakness. Other managers would like to educate their employees, to make them more knowledgeable, but because they sense no loyalty to the workplace, they feel it simply costs too much to invest in people who will leave for a better offer tomorrow. Is it any wonder then, that sometimes organizations take the easy way out and say their workforce is knowledgeable when, in reality, what their workforce has been given is only some carefully selected information?

The danger in mislabeling information as knowledge is that once someone who has information is labeled as knowledgeable, the expectations change. We expect that person to behave as a knowledgeable person when in reality, he or she might lack the education and wisdom—the broader information—to react to data in a productive fashion. For the information/knowledge symbiosis to be complete, both elements—information and knowledge—must be present. Why do we continue to be surprised when we provide loads of information, but projects fail anyway? And how do we expect our workers to be empowered if they don't have the opportunities to become knowledgeable?

An organization that gives lip service to the word "empowerment" needs to take some time for self-examination. Is management threatened by the idea that an employee might know more than is absolutely necessary to do his or her job? Are employees fed information on a need to know basis? Are employee questions answered with, "That's not in your job description?" If so, the organization could be deluding itself about how empowered, or how knowledgeable, the workforce really is.

Clearly, there are circumstances where an employee needs to focus on his or her own area instead of trying to swim in someone else's pond. And often, there are proprietary secrets that must be protected. Premature publication of a projected product launch date, for example, could be devastating for a company. I am not proposing an open book policy, but I am proposing that management include people in the information stream as much as possible. Let employees see the larger picture so they have the knowledge to recognize how their work fits into the whole and can therefore make better decisions about the data they encounter.

It is true that knowledge is power. So many managers seem to think that power is something to be held onto and kept from employees. Why not empower the employees with knowledge so that the entire organization is powerful instead?

In her book, *Leadership and the New Science: Learning About Organization From an Orderly Universe*, Margaret Wheatley takes a look at what can happen when information is allowed to flow freely in an organization. In fact, she encourages people and teams to become so overloaded with information, it seems nothing can be understood from it. Her thought is that disorganized information will begin to organize around a new thought or process that has never before been imagined.

This approach is a complete contradiction to the "need to know" mentality. It recognizes each employee as a possible inspiration generator. How threatening words such as, "chaos," "disorganized," "random" and "non-linear" must sound to organizational managers. Yet these words are at the root of new ideas and empowerment.

Management by *knowledge* recognizes the unique spiritual and intellectual needs and potentials of the individual. It is education and information about the job and how it relates to other areas of the organization. It supports increased productivity and creativity. Management by *information* lets employees know what is expected of them and defines the limits of their authority. It relates to policies, rules and regulations, job descriptions and expectations. It is the opposite of empowerment.

SKILLS AND ABILITIES

It is easy for management to sit back and say, "If we didn't think that person could do the job, we wouldn't give them the responsibility." But is that enough? Is it saying that, theoretically, the person *could* do the job? Is that saying that compared to the other candidates this person came *closest* to being able to the do the job?

In an empowering organization, management constantly keeps an eye on skill development. Instead of training people only to do the job for which they are currently employed, management also considers the specific skills for the job the employee *might* do. This means creative leaders must look beyond the confines of traditional job descriptions and see the true *spirit* of work itself. Empowered organizations train employees for where they are going and not just where they are now.

Additional responsibility is something that can be planned for and practiced. It is part of what keeps an employee growing in the job. It is part of what makes an employee feel empowered in the workplace. "There is a future here," he or she can say. "The company believes in me." Have you ever heard a manager bemoan, "I can't get my employees to stop taking responsibility for things?" Of course not, so why do we work so hard to discourage and limit responsibility by confining our employees to rigidly defined tasks?

Ask yourself what your organization would look like if every employee knew what to do, when, how, where to do it, and why. Such organizations exist, but for many, it almost sounds Utopian, doesn't it? Imagine how efficient such an organization might be. If an organization believes itself to be empowering, but isn't running with that model in place, perhaps empowerment is only a word being tossed around in meetings. Perhaps the leadership is confusing accountability with empowerment.

ATTITUDE

Much of an employee's ability to take on new responsibility, or to even perform their current task well, is lumped under the heading of attitude. This is not a mislabeling. I would simply like to break it down a little further.

Attitude is more than an employee feeling good about the job. In fact, I believe that too much emphasis in recent years has been placed on employee feelings without enough analysis of what's really being talked about. Law firms collect checks because some employee felt "icky" in the workplace. People turn to litigation simply because someone made them feel bad. Our society has identified feeling good all the time as a reasonable expectation, and if it isn't met, someone needs to pay! I ask, where is the responsibility of the individual for his or her own feelings?

Empowerment and addressing the spiritual nature of our workforce is not about feelings. True, the result of empowerment can be wonderfully positive feelings, but to mistake feeling good as the end goal of good management is to miss the point. It is not the employer's duty to put a smile on the face of every employee. Employees need to appear at the job willing and able to put the smile there themselves. It is the employer's responsibility to treat employees humanely, with respect, and to give them the opportunity to grow spiritually and mentally, and to thereby feel good about their work and enjoy it. Feeling good is the byproduct of the effort, not the focus of the effort. The employer can create the environment, and must; but ultimately the individuals must accept responsibility for their own feelings and for the fact that growth is not always easy or fun.

Organizations who throw benefits and wages and all sorts of flexibility at their employees without addressing the deeper spiritual forces at work in human nature are trying to buy good behavior. Granted, these "motivators" might be the result of collective bargaining, but they still miss the boat. It's like parents who overindulge and spoil their children. The child might smile in satisfaction at all the goodies he or she receives, but the smile is only temporary, and he or she feels no need to contribute to the family in any worthwhile way. The child might have power, but there is no empowerment.

I have seen organizations lose all sense of direction and purpose—their focus on quality flying out the window— in their attempt to ensure that their employees felt good. They mistook this for empowerment, and while the confusion is understandable—both approaches describe "happy" employees—the feel-good focus is a shortcut that bypasses the spiritual aspect of the workplace and ultimately leads to disaster. Pacified employees are not necessarily productive employees. Employees can feel good about producing a product, but there might not be any customers who want to buy it. We must be careful what we label empowerment. It is easy to grow complacent when everyone is behaving.

Part of empowerment is communicating reasonable expectations. It is part stretching the individual and part guiding and rewarding him or her. It is acknowledgement of a job well done and the support to be sure the job can be done well.

An empowered attitude is much more about thinking good than feeling good, and this goes back to the difference between knowledge and information. A knowledgeable employee sees the big picture and believes in the mission of the organization. With that knowledge, the employee focuses on the work and results and takes the necessary responsibility. There is more at stake for that individual than whether he or she can "get another piece of candy" from an employer.

Empowered employees know that they make a difference, and they know how to make a difference. They know that their company values them and stands behind them. They don't buy into the present mythology of victimization that holds the workplace accountable for their good day. They take credit for their good days themselves and are thus likely to have more of them.

Obviously, if an organization is mistreating its employees or breaking the law, it must be held accountable in our legal system. I believe this strongly. But perhaps our society has gone too far in expecting a smooth career path. The employees need to pull their share of the load, too. Empowered employees with the skills to succeed exhibit them in their attitudes toward other employees, their employers and their work.

AUTHORITY

One of the often overlooked aspects of the empowered workplace is the clear communication of authority. Unlike a job description, which lists a number of tasks that define and confine the job, this communication is about enabling employees to react and make judgments as situations arise.

Do the employees understand the scope of their responsibilities and do they have adequate authority to carry out this responsibility? This communication could vary from establishing a budget for expenditures to letting the receptionist know that he or she can tell a manager that some typing has to wait if the phones are too busy.

Any time an employee is given responsibility for a task without the authority to ensure its success, the manager needs to do some soul-searching. The project manager who is not allowed to hold a difficult team member accountable for his or her work; the employee who has to complete a project while pretending that the supervisor is doing the work; and the understaffed customer service director who is evaluated based on customer satisfaction, but who may not hire more personnel to provide a quick response time, are all examples of employees who are being used and used up by their employers because the employers will not give them the authority and power to do what is expected of them.

Managers put employees in these situations for a variety of reasons. And it happens frequently. Sometimes it's oversight, but all too often, it has to do with the manager's weakness or self-absorption. A manager who skips a careful evaluation of the authority aspect of empowerment while doling out additional responsibility and calling it empowerment is lying to himself about his effect on the workplace.

Empowerment has become a big word in the management world, but it is easily confused with other things. Roget's Thesaurus describes empowerment as "to enable and endow, to authorize and invest with power, to switch on."

Wouldn't it be wonderful if we could truly learn to switch on the American workforce?

We walk on the beach, looking for bright,

shiny treasures, when our true wealth is the

supportive sand already beneath our feet.

KEEP YOUR EYE ON THE PRIZE – THE CUSTOMER IS EVERYTHING

"I want you to walk away knowing two things. First, the customer is the boss. Second, the three most important words you'll ever hear from a customer, 'I'll be back.'"

Robert E. Farrell,
Author of *Give 'Em The Pickle* and
founder of Farrell's Ice Cream Parlours

Sometimes, in all the interpretation of analysis, identification of objectives, and massaging of the organizational structure, we forget why we exist as organizations. Is it not that at some point in time, there was a need to be met and we saw an opportunity to meet that need? Whomever our customers are, do we not exist because of them? It seems to me that some managers think organizations exist only to give them someplace to advance their personal agendas. And, some front-line employees behave as though employers exist only to dole out paychecks.

I can't help but think that most companies begin with a wonderful vision of what they want to be. Included in this vision is a complete commitment to the customer, but something happens along the way. All the things related to running the company get in the way of the fundamental dynamic. The customer becomes the result of the product and not the reason for it. I believe that many companies fail because they lose sight of this one simple element: pleasing the customer is the most important thing.

I want to tell you a story. I had a friend tell me that he gave my name to an organization that was interested in a strategic planning project. He told me the culture was opinionated, dedicated, headstrong, somewhat scattered and headed by a director who had set a very high bar for all his staff to clear. After asking my friend a few questions, I wondered if I really wanted to get involved with these people. I decided a general meeting with the director couldn't hurt, and if I didn't feel comfortable, I could always recommend someone else.

At the first meeting, we started out with some pleasantries. Then I began to ask some general questions about the company's products and attitudes. Finally, I asked the director what he saw as their biggest issue. His reply started to move me immediately into his corner.

The director stated, "We're losing sight of our customers. Something has happened to our focus. We've become so hung up on being a company that we are starting to take things for granted. I think it's more than just training. Something is dying."

I asked him what he wanted to achieve as a result of the strategic planning. He looked at me straight in the eye and said, "We need to know what we want to be when we grow up."

I was hooked. I immediately wanted to be part of the process to help this company get back in focus. Over the next few months we concentrated on issues and on setting priorities for the company. The employees rose to the occasion and gave their input eagerly, holding nothing back. We had a great time. It was as if everyone had been waiting for a chance to re-energize and re-commit.

One critical issue on which we focused was identifying and renewing the company's core values, among which was the recognition that the customer is at the center of the company purpose. It was invigorating. We set up a process by which all projects have to link to a core value. Suddenly, the employees knew where the ship was headed and they were all eager for their turn at the oars. Relationships with customers and customer satisfaction became a daily priority. From this step alone, of re-attaching to the fundamentals, things began to turn around. Moving on from there was easy. The groundwork was already laid.

CUSTOMER INTERACTION—CURSE OR OPPORTUNITY?

Haven't we all been served by customer service personnel who view customer contact as an inconvenience? I always marvel at the front-line people who don't serve the customer with joy. After all, where would their jobs be if the customers weren't there?

Let me relate a personal experience. I went to apply for my vehicle license tags for a two-year renewal. I went to a branch office of the Department of Motor Vehicles and found two other customers who were already being served and a third open window behind which a man was slowly shuffling some papers. There was nobody else waiting, and I assumed I would be next. Not one of the three clerks looked up at me or acknowledged my presence in any way. Finally, I noticed a machine with a sign that said "Take A Number." It seemed a little silly, but I took a number, number 56, and sat down in the waiting area. I waited. I waited some more. Still, none of the clerks even glanced my way.

When one of the customers left, I watched the now free clerk leisurely finish some paperwork, straighten his area and, almost against his will, turn to look at the large LCD panel that glowed with the red number 56.

"Number 56," I heard him call. Still no eye contact.

When I approached the counter and explained what I needed, the clerk proceeded to strike up a conversation with the clerk next to him about basketball. I had to interrupt his conversation to ask a few questions.

At no time did I feel I was more than number 56 to him. I was not a client, customer, or even a person. I was number 56 and forgettable. This person probably knew everything there was to know about taking care of DMV paperwork. He was trained, methodical, and precise. And, he didn't know a thing about his job. He was working for a public service agency and acting as though he was doing me a favor.

I believe that if the State intended for their DMV clerks to be this impersonal, they'd put machines in the mall where I'd insert my money and get my vehicle tags. The term "public service" is not supposed to be an oxymoron.

So what went wrong? Surely the clerk doesn't remember number 56 from March 29, 1999, but I remember! And, fair or not, it affects my view of his organization. Obviously, there are some individuals who simply shouldn't be in contact with customers. They don't have the aptitude or ability to serve customers directly. But sometimes, entire departments develop a negative customer attitude. The lack of service is widespread and the customers are quick to notice. It can be devastating for a company, and unfortunately, management might never realize why sales have suddenly dropped.

Where is the education and larger perspective that makes front-line employees see their role as a critical function for the success of the company? And if they do realize their own importance to the organization, why don't they care? Where is the spirit of leadership that models customer contact as an opportunity to gather information about how to better serve the customer in the future?

I would point the finger at the attitude of the leadership. Clearly, if the leadership in an organization does not have a personal commitment to customer service, we can't expect the front-line employees to have one, but I think it goes beyond that. I think it has to do with the way information flows within the company. Information flow should be the natural order of things, and yet organizations go out of their way to inhibit, control and use information as power. I see information as nourishment for the employee. Employees who are given a constant supply of information, and the knowledge to apply it, can make all the difference in an organization's ability to maintain a meaningful customer relationship.

Also, if information about the customers from those who have immediate contact with them can't flow up the information chain, not only is the organization losing valuable feedback, but the front-line employees themselves will have no reason to ideologically and emotionally invest in the organization.

Sometimes, the front-line employees are the lowest paid; in some industries that means only minimum wage. Wage can be a factor, but I've worked with many companies that pay minimum wage, yet the managers listen, and the employees grow, provide input, and participate in the success of the company. If employees are nurtured spiritually through their work, it makes all the difference. Unless an employee is treated as an intrinsic and valuable part of the team, with a mind and ability, it is hard to expect anything more than low wages performance.

I am always surprised to find situations where customer service is weak. If customer satisfaction is what drives the success of the organization, why do some organizations invest so little effort in educating, supporting, and listening to, the front-line people who represent the company to the customer?

The Effect of Quotas and Performance Objectives on the Customer

Some people love numbers. They want to quantify every action in the organization so it can be evaluated and analyzed and used to develop new target numbers. There is value to this process. Numbers and statistics help us condense information into meaningful data that can help us guide the organization to greater success. Statistical process tools, which come out of the process, instead of being applied to it, are invaluable.

The problem arises for the customer when the numbers are generated just to have numbers. Quotas and performance measures have the insidious ability to make us feel in control when in reality the ship might be sinking. Sometimes, they are even what's causing the water to come in.

It is easy to lose sight of the larger target when we set smaller arbitrary targets and hold employees accountable for meeting them. For example, would it make sense for a sales force to have a customer contact quota that forced them to call on people who weren't reasonable prospects? It happens. Someone in a meeting somewhere decides that if we're going to increase sales, we need to increase contacts and therefore sets a new contact quota. If the goal is stated as "contact this many new people or you won't get your bonus" instead of "find out what customers need and want," the employee is going to do what it takes to survive even while losing respect, and attachment to, the organization.

I see two dangers in the overuse of performance objectives and quotas. First, they dehumanize the employees, reducing them to number-producing machines. Second, it often means that the managers are so lost in the process and lofty ideas that they've forgotten to include the customer in the equation. We end up with organizations that appear to be productive on paper, but don't meet the needs of the customers. I can see management scratching their heads when their achievements don't add up to profit on the income statement.

Bennet Cerf, founder of Random House Publishing, was invited to tour the plant of a large New York paper mill that supplied most of the paper to the New York publishing industry. The sales manager and his sales representatives provided a tour of the plant and hosted a lavish reception to woo publisher business.

The food was excellent and the wine and beverages flowed freely throughout the evening. The sales manager rose to his feet and with a catch in his voice said, "Just fifteen years ago today our mill received its very first paper order from a book publisher."

A front-line salesman at the rear of the room piped up: "And when are you going to fill it?"

He might have asked instead, "When are we going to start serving the customer?" It is easy to have a goal of "making lots of sales." Maybe the sales force for this paper company was good at it. But if that is the corporate goal, what happens to the energy and resources? They get directed to making sales, not filling orders. If the goal doesn't involve serving the customers, the business can't be sustained because management will forget to take care of business. They'll be so focused on speeding ahead that they'll ignore the icebergs of poor service that lurk beneath the surface.

THE MOVING TARGET

Sometimes the icebergs aren't about productivity and service. The customer changes. For decades, Swiss watchmakers had the world market for watches sewn up because they produced a high quality product that was in demand. Customer loyalty was assumed. Then came the electronic quartz movement. Companies around the world, especially in Japan, leapt on the new technology and the Swiss were left behind. The problem for the Swiss was not that they stopped producing good watches; it was that their customers' desires changed. The only way an organization can survive such a shift is to constantly keep the customer in view. It is another reason why feedback from the front line is so critical. You can't force the customer to stay the same. Customers don't care about how things were always done before and they don't care about how you feel. The customer only cares about how you think and if your thinking produces a benefit for them.

SOLUTION

I believe it comes down to "thinking good." Management needs to educate and inspire employees to focus on the customer. We need to evaluate our processes and production goals to ensure that they keep the customer in view. We need to keep information about customers flowing in all directions. If the customer impact is not at the heart of evaluating productivity, you can end up with motivated, productive people being held accountable for a dysfunctional system. Beating the numbers from last month, or somebody else's numbers, is only better if the customer benefits.

If we keep this focus on the customer, many of the other facets of the workplace environment will fall into place.

It is no secret that it's difficult to turn out a quality product with a workforce that is disillusioned and isolated. While it's difficult to quantify with numbers and bar graphs, every employee in an organization has an idea of how that culture is performing at the spiritual level, and whether there is a sense of pride in the product or any concern about the customer. The customer is best served by a workplace environment where employees are valued, heeded, and included. It is a workplace that sees the heart and soul as the most valuable resource available. Keep the customer in mind and the workplace can flourish.

COMMUNICATION TRANSCENDS LANGUAGE

AND OUR ABILITY TO SPEAK. IT IS NOT TEACHING

SOMEONE THE POWER OF ONE AND ONE.

COMMUNICATION IS TEACHING THE POWER OF 'AND.'

COMMUNICATION

*Crisis in dialogue occurs when the participants...fail to really address
each other but turn away defensively, each within himself, for the
purposes of self-justification."*

Reuel Howe
American Theologian

What is communication? On the surface, we say
we communicate to draw people together to share
ideas, information, or a point of view. We might
want to know what the other person is thinking, to know what
that person knows. Or, we might simply want to get the other
side to see things our way.

I see true communication as a spiritual process, a reforming
of some aspect of ourselves into a new way of being. It is a willingness to change ourselves and our point of view if the circumstance dictates change. More than the ability to organize our
thoughts and transmit them, communication is also the courage
to receive new knowledge and respond to it. It is the willingness

to have ideas flow in two directions. It is stepping into the unknown.

For many people in management, those to whom control and the appearance of knowing everything is paramount, this point of view is unacceptable. "How can I lead if I don't know all the answers?" they ask.

George Fox, the founder of the Quaker movement, faced this same challenge. In the early stages of his ministry, he encountered many people who were seeking a new way. They wanted something different, but nobody knew quite what that was. They needed leadership into the unknown, not someone who already knew all the answers.

According to Robert Greenleaf, in his book *Servant Leadership*, Fox employed two principles worth noting. First, he truly communicated with his seekers, and in doing so created an environment where the unknown was not only acceptable, but welcome. Second, he created a group structure in which each member could feel comfortable. Feeling safe within the group and learning to trust the process enabled Fox and his followers to freely explore the needs of the group and to clearly establish their priorities and belief systems. Greenleaf also relates that the root of the word "religion" is *religio*, meaning to rebind. Fox's communication leadership helped his followers *rebind* their beliefs, resulting in a new form of worship and a new way of life.

While we aren't founding a new religion, we can learn from

Fox's example. Our workers need to have faith in the process and trust their leaders to lead them into the unknown. With leadership, the future becomes exciting and important. With faith in the structure, and with true communication, employees begin to trust the system enough to identify it with themselves. They see their values in harmony with the organization and with other individuals within the organization. They begin to see their unique contributions to the tasks at hand. They buy into the communal workplace purpose and as a result, find satisfaction and fulfillment in their jobs.

With true communication, leaders in the workplace can make the unknown welcome, as George Fox did, and rebind disorganization and fragmented information into something new and more vibrant, which benefits both the organization and the people in it.

One way to think of communication is to think of an equation. In mathematics, we use the plus sign (+) to show how two amounts are added together to become a different amount. In communication, the plus sign can become the symbol for growth, for balancing life's equations. If I take my own life experiences and add (+) another person's point of view, I have the opportunity to move to the other side of the equal sign (=) to see what the outcome will be. With true communication, both sides have the choice to balance their own equation. Instead of one side winning and one side losing, both sides can win.

So often, when we don't like what someone says, we close them off and circle the wagons of self-interest. This is understandable and human, but think of the barriers we throw up to justify our personal opinion. In fact, stop for a moment and think of that last time you circled your own wagons. Was there a way you could have helped the outcome of that transaction be more balanced? Was there information you could have integrated into your own viewpoint had you been able to participate in true communication in that instance?

We have to remember, when communicating, that we can be stubborn and win the battle of getting what we want, but with patience, tact, and consideration we might instead get what we really need.

I believe that the human spirit seeks this process of true communication, but because we fear the unknown, or just out of habit, we often keep ourselves from realizing our communicative potential. What can we do to better understand our personal communication style and, if we're too often circling the wagons and not balancing the equation, how can we begin to move toward a truer method of communicating? I offer three steps:

INVENTORY YOUR ATTITUDE

What are the issues that you put in the way of effective communication?

Robert Bennett in his book, *Gaining Control*, gives a great example of belief windows. He shares how Mother Teresa looked at the world through her belief window and resolved to serve the poorest of the poor regardless of her own personal condition. A belief window at the opposite end of the spectrum would be that of members of the Ku Klux Klan. Their view of the poor, and of racial boundaries and ethnic origin are quite different from Mother Teresa's, but the attitudes and behaviors of both Mother Teresa and the Ku Klux Klan evince strong beliefs.

Now, your work environment might not induce behaviors at such opposite ends of the spectrum as those of Mother Teresa or the KKK, but we do need to analyze how our belief systems affect our response to the issues which confront us. Are we open to true communication, or are we more interested in perpetuating a power group? If you are circling your wagons on a daily basis, it might be life-changing to ask yourself, "Why?"

Maybe we use guilt or the ever-faithful anger to build fences in our lives to keep ourselves from moving forward and accepting change. Knowing our feelings does not necessarily move us forward. It is a step, but it is not the solution. Think of all those times when we have used our feelings as a barrier that kept us from communicating or making decisions. Hiding behind our feelings becomes comfortable, safe, and non-threatening, but it can also be crippling.

Inhibiting communication and not looking at what we have written on our belief window, due to guilt, fear, or anger, makes us static. We respond to our feelings and look no farther, hiding—at least from ourselves—the real issues at hand. The "feelings game" becomes a form of complacency, and the first victims of complacency are communication and growth.

We have tainted several generations with the absurd notion that being in touch with our feelings will get us through life's problems. Recognizing our feelings is an important step, but the next step needs to be taken. Changing our thinking, and being accountable for our actions is the other side of the "feelings" equation. It is only when we become responsible for our side of the interaction that we can expect to truly communicate.

ISOLATE THE INTERRUPTERS

What issues interrupt you the most? Write them down and then prioritize them. Find out what stumbling blocks you might be putting in the way of effective communication and connection. What might some of the interrupters be? Ask yourself:

- Am I afraid of failure or success?
- Do I get angry when I am challenged or asked to justify my position?
- Do I raise my voice when I want to make a point?

- Do I use silence to avoid dealing with issues?
- Do I use accusations to turn a conversation away from a point of view?
- Do I use my own guilt to accuse others?

Write down what thinking process might be behind your interrupters. When do you employ them? Do you use them to avoid taking responsibility for a position? Are you avoiding change? If you want to change the interrupters, you must change the thinking process that created them.

It seems to me that the root issue is often fear. I believe the two biggest barriers to communication are the fear of failure and fear of success. Let's look at this more closely.

Our culture looks upon failure as a bad grade on the report card of life. So what if we fail at something? Life is not lived just at C+ and above. What an absurd notion that you have to succeed at everything to be acceptable. The world is full of people who do not have a college education, for example, who have overcome the interrupters of life, addressed fear, embraced wisdom and communicated their way to success. A turtle could keep his head tucked in his shell all his life, but it's only by sticking his neck out that he ever gets anywhere.

Success can be just as frightening. Success attracts attention. It puts us in the spotlight and forces us to constantly have to live up to our own prior achievements. Depending on where you are in an organization, success in most endeavors not only will get you noticed, it will also get you more work. Yes, this can be good, but it is also a price one pays. Whichever fear you choose, failure or success, the results you get are yours. You cannot blame them on anyone else.

MOVE TO A HIGHER LEVEL

Set a personal and professional standard. Make it a point to listen to those people you consider leaders. Don't look at the opportunity as a random occurrence. Plan opportunities. Watch and learn until positive leadership becomes part of your belief window. Rebind your thoughts with positive actions and principles. Get beyond just hearing. Learn to listen.

Listening requires commitment to understanding the other person's point of view. It doesn't mean you have to agree, it means that you have to keep digging until you *understand.* It means thinking with resolve and conviction, not blindly responding to an unrecognized or unresolved emotion.

True communication is principle-centered living. It requires a clear set of governing values being lived out in daily life. Stephen Covey in the book, *First Things First,* relates the goal of life is to live, love, learn, and leave a legacy. Principle-centered living requires us to acknowledge the fear of failure or success. It is when we no longer have to fear learning another point of view in an exchange of ideas. We have the choice to see the world more clearly and to communicate in a positive and directed fashion.

Attitude is everything. Attitude is the acceptance of who we are and the deep and penetrating resolve of honoring internal values.

When we become leaders who have the courage to communicate, a whole new spectrum of possibilities awaits us and the organizations in which we work. To grow and flourish in the new millennium, the American workplace must establish new habits of communication. The time to start is now. And whatever positions we hold in the workplace, the place to begin is within each of us.

THE CHALLENGE FACING WORKING AMERICA

IS TO RETURN THE DIGNITY OF THE HUMAN SPIRIT TO THE

WORKPLACE SO IT IS THERE FOR OUR CHILDREN.

WE HAVE ABANDONED OUR HEARTS AND SOULS TO THE

SIN OF COMPROMISE.

Managing in the New Millennium

"The rotting fish begins to stink at the head."

Italian proverb

Each Human Spirit

We all recognize the speed at which our world is changing, and nothing is changing faster than our customer. Our organizational ships are cutting through the water at ever faster rates. Necessary course corrections will have to occur long before we are accustomed to looking for them, because the faster rate of change won't give us as much time to react. It's a high-pressure world and the seas in which we sail can be unforgiving.

Until now, the obvious reaction to this fast-paced, shifting, and sometimes brutal environment was to be sure that the boats—our companies—were equipped with the latest technology. Upgrade the equipment and the boat will sail faster, right? That works, to a point. But even in elite yacht races, it is not necessarily the fastest boat that wins, it is the fast boat with the best crew.

In such a race, every member of the crew is working to his or her full potential. The captain depends on the team to react quickly and surely. They are trained and coached, and know how critical each role is for the success of the team. If there's an unforeseen crisis, the captain knows that his crew is creative and knowledgeable and can adapt to the changing circumstances effectively. There is only one captain, but those winning the races also have an empowered, spirited crew.

The days of buying up the latest technology, plunking it down in front of the employees and then holding them accountable for the success of the company are over. Technology without knowledge and leadership doesn't get the job done. There has to be a leader, empowered inspired employees, and a team commitment to winning the race.

The wonderful paradox of these times is that to solve the problems of the new workplace, we have to return to the oldest of values. We have to nurture the part of us that has never become obsolete, despite our attempts to mold it, deny it, or stamp it out of existence. We have to return to recognizing the human spirit. Unless we begin to acknowledge the humanity in all of us and realize how critical the spiritual effects of the workplace are to the success of the organization, we are doomed to failure.

The symptoms of our lack of spiritual awareness in the workplace are all around us. People are frustrated, anxious, and angry, and the effects of this unhappiness are seen in domestic violence, road rage, and now, even employee violence in the workplace. The effects are seen on the bottom lines of the income statements of corporate America.

Management complains about employee attitudes and how much it costs to buy their satisfaction. They forget what it costs them in productivity and turnover when employees are unhappy. And, unfortunately, everyone forgets that employee satisfaction is much more than a benefits/policies package. What employees need, and what employers so often fail to give them is so simple. It is the institutional and personal valuing of the human spirit.

This is a turnaround for many of us, a totally foreign concept. It is antithetical to the training we receive in our MBA programs and it is certainly not what we usually think about in the trenches of corporate warfare. But it is the secret to the future. This new approach is not only moral and uplifting, it will become necessary. The circumstances of the new millennium will require this change from us.

THE SHAPE OF THINGS TO COME

The new organizations of the millennium will eliminate the autocratic fiefdoms of the old system. They will work outside of the boxes of organizational charts and job descriptions. They will deliberately seek out new lines of communication and will let knowledge flow throughout the organization. The tall trees, the leaders, will shelter all of the diverse elements of the organization so it can flourish and achieve sustained growth, instead of focusing on the short-term harvest. The mission statements will be clear and based in a universal ethic. Every decision will be run through the litmus test of customer benefit, and new goals will be established based on what is happening within the entire organization, instead of being based on departmental politics.

The new organizations will recognize that they are always in motion. They will be adaptive and flexible. Creativity will be prized at all levels. In the future, organizations will be viewed as an assembly of personal skills instead of a set of traditional business units.

As we move into the new mentality, we will learn to nurture the dreamers and will recognize that an employee can only be as effective as the system lets him or her be. We will create an environment where employees can learn, grow, risk, fail, discover, and have faith in what they are doing.

People want to believe in what they are doing. They want to proudly include their work life as a statement of who they are. Even the lowest paid employees in the chain can have this benefit if they are given the knowledge to understand how they fit into the system.

These ideas about the spirit and the workplace are not really new to us. They are grounded in Judeo-Christian traditions. Haven't we all heard about the Protestant Work Ethic? It addresses the spirit in the sense of accomplishment in an honest day's work, and then recognizes the importance of the Sabbath to rejuvenate spiritually for the week ahead. The rule St. Benedict established in the 5th century makes it clear that we have a spiritual relationship to work. "Work is prayer, and prayer is work," he said. Judaism emphasizes this in yet another way, making an unmistakable connection between human spirituality and all of our endeavors.

It is no surprise that the seven needs for personal productivity in the workplace are essentially spiritual. Our work is a huge part of our journey; therefore, it will have a spiritual impact on us whether for the good or otherwise. The recognition of this one fact will transform the American workplace in the new millennium and can, as a result, foster hope and faith for each human spirit.

APPENDIX

A CHECKLIST FOR TRANSFORMATION

- Continuously evaluate your management selection process.
- Teach leadership within the organization. In larger companies, create a leadership track that supports continuous education in leadership skills and communicates leadership expectations.
- Make communication a priority for management, both at the interpersonal level and in more formal settings.
- Train leaders in understanding the spiritual and emotional needs of the workforce. Include psychological elements and the Seven Needs for Personal Productivity.
- Establish a tone of openness and be willing to be shaken up by new ideas.
- Train leaders to use statistical process tools so that all of the interdependent facets of the organization are working in harmony.
- Do not tolerate destructive, expensive management behaviors.
- Establish a strong mission statement and keep it in the forefront of decision-making.
- Keep the customer in view in all things.

Applying the Seven Needs for Personal Productivity to Your Life

While I developed the seven needs primarily for application to the workplace, I have found over the years that they can serve as a good checklist for decision-making and evaluation in the rest of our twenty-four hour lives as well. By changing the focus slightly, we can adapt them to almost any situation. In this appendix are three examples of how you might do this.

I repeat the seven needs here for your reference:

1. Your work must have meaning.

2. You must have input into your destiny.

3. You must be paid a fair wage.

4. Your work must add quality to your life.

5. Your work must bring meaningful relationships to your life.

6. Your work must provide variety in what you do.

7. Your work must be viewed as important.

For the first example, let's say we must deal with an ill parent or relative who needs to be placed in a care facility of some kind. This is often an extremely difficult decision to make, and our fear of making a wrong choice can be paralyzing. As you assess the different facilities, consider each of the seven needs as a basis for interviewing each care provider.

Here are some examples:

1. What is the mission of your organization? How do you fulfill it?

2. How do residents provide input and how are such requests or suggestions addressed?

3. How does your facility and care compare with similar organizations? What sets you apart?

4. How does this facility address quality of life issues for your residents and how does the facility work to enhance quality of life?

5. What opportunities do residents have for positive social interaction?

6. Do you have programs for education, entertainment, or the pursuit of special interests?

7. How are residents made to feel important?

You might also want to look at the seven needs in light of your interactions with your family if you have children. Here are some examples of how you might apply the seven needs to set parenting goals for yourself:

1. Help my child find meaning and purpose in life.

2. Listen to my child's point of view and let him or her have appropriate input into his or her destiny.

3. Provide an adequate lifestyle where his or her basic physical needs are met, plus provide the emotional components for well-being.

4. Guide my child to interests and activities and relationships that enhance his or her quality of life.

5. Provide unconditional and unquestioned love.

6. Provide a model for lifelong learning in the emotional, spiritual, and intellectual realms.

7. Show my child through my actions that he or she is an important member of the family.

Finally, we can use the seven needs for self-examination.

1. What are the important things in life?

2. Am I using my spiritual beliefs to help me set my course?

3. Do I have a plan for reaching my goals? Am I actively pursuing them?

4. Am I living in a way that enables me to thrive spiritually and emotionally?

5. Am I connecting with, and contributing to, the people around me?

6. Am I learning? Am I growing?

7. Do I make a positive difference in the world, even if it is a small one?

Understanding the Seven Needs for Personal Productivity isn't the only key to finding meaning and fulfillment in the workplace or in our personal life. But you can see by these examples that they can serve as a quick checklist to see if we are going in the right direction.

Also, while we can't expect any situation to fully satisfy all of these needs, it seems important that we keep striving toward that end. We must nurture our own spiritual needs and provide for the needs of others around us, whether it is in our families, in the community, or in the workplace.

RECOMMENDED READING

Allen, James, **As A Man Thinketh: Classics of Inspiration,** Kansas City, Hallmark Cards, Inc., 1968

Anderson, Nancy, **Work With Passion: How To Do What You Love For Living,** Carroll and Graf Publishers, New World Library, 1995

Belasco, James A., Ph.D, **Teaching The Elephant To Dance: The Managers Guide to Empowering Change,** New York, Penguin Books, 1990

Bennett, Robert, Kurt Hanks, and Gerreld L. Pulsipher, **Gaining Control,** Salt Lake City, Franklin International Institute, Inc., 1987

Cheaney, Lee andMaury Cotter, **Real People Real Work: Parables on Leadership in the '90s,** Knoxville, Tenn., SPC Press, 1991

Covey, Stephen R., A. Roger Merrill, and Rebecca R. Merrill, **First Things First,** New York, Simon & Schuster, 1994

Covey, Stephen R., **Principle-Centered Leadership,** New York, Simon & Schuster, 1993

Deming. W. Edwards, **Out of the Crisis,** Massachusetts Institute of Technology Press, 2000

Deming. W. Edwards, **The New Economics For Business, Government And Education,** Massachusetts Institute of Technology Center for Advanced Engineering Study, 1993

DePree, Max, *Leadership Is An Art,* New York, Dell Publishing, 1989

The Bible

The Torah

Eigen, Lewis D., and Jonathan P. Siegel, *Management Book Of Quotations,* New York, American Management Association, 1989

Frankl, Victor E., *Man's Search For Meaning: An Introduction To Logotherapy,* New York, Simon & Schuster, 1998

Greenleaf, Robert, *Servant Leadership: A Journey Into the Nature of Power and Greatness,* New York, Paulist Press, 1991

Levoy, Gregg, *Callings: Finding and Following An Authentic Life,* New York, Simon & Schuster, 1998

Merton, Thomas, *The Ascent To Truth*, New York, Harcourt Brace Jovanovich, 1951, 1979

Merton, Thomas, *New Seeds Of Contemplation,* New York, New Directions Publishing Corporation, 1962

Oakley, Ed and Doug Krug, *Enlightened Leadership: Getting to the Heart of Change,* New York, Simon & Schuster, 1991

Ritzer, George, *The McDonaldization Of Society*, Thousand Oaks, California, Pine Forge Press, A Sage Publications Company, 1993

Ryan, Kathleen D. and Daniel K. Oestreich, *Driving Fear From the Workplace: How To Overcome the Invisible Barriers to Quality, Productivity, and Innovation,* San Francisco, Jossey-Bass Publishers, 1991

Sinetar, Marsha, *Do What You Love, The Money Will Follow: Discovering Your Right Livelihood*, New York, Dell Publishing, 1987

Scherkenbach, William W., *Deming's Road To Continual Improvement*, Knoxville, Tennessee, SPC Press, Inc.,1991

Wheeler, Donald J. *Understanding Variation: The Key To Managing Chaos,* Knoxville, Tennessee, SPC Press, Inc., 2000

Wheatley, Margaret, *Leadership And The New Science; Learning About Organization From an Orderly Universe,* San Francisco, Berrett- Kohler Publishers, 1992

Whitney, John, *Economics Of Trust: Liberating Profits And Restoring Corporate Vitality,* New York, McGraw-Hill, 1996

Wubbolding, Robert, Ed.D., *Employee Motivation: What to Do When What You Say Isn't Working,* Knoxville, Tennessee, SPC Press, Inc., 1996

Zenger, John, Ed Mussellwhite, Kathleen Hurson, and Craig Verrin, *Leading Teams: Mastering the New Role,* Homewood, Illinois, Book Press, Inc., Business One Irwin, 1993

Index

J

jealousy 76, 144
job descriptions 58, 169–173, 180, 186, 187, 194, 196, 200
Judaism 229
Judeo-Christian traditions 229

K

knowledge 173, 192–195, 215, 226
  as power 54, 194
    see also data, information
knowledge management 181
    see also information; knowledge
Krejci, Frank 49–51, 73
Ku Klux Klan 219

L

loyalty 17, 21, 37, 48, 50, 66, 90-92, 109, 114, 138, 150, 193, 211
  see *also* disloyalty

M

 meaning in work 18–20, 36, 172
meaningful relationships 27–28, 37
meetings 150–152
Mellon, Andrew 44
memos 83, 120, 171
mentor 23, 74, 87, 110, 125, 126
Mr. Magoo 86
money, as motivator 22, 154–156, 185
Mother Teresa 15, 219
motivation 66, 74, 99, 176, 183.
  long term 157–158, 159
  short term 154–157, 159
    see also money, as motivator

N

non-monetary compensation
  see fair wage; motivation
numbers 51, 66–69, 112–113, 145–146, 173–176, 177–179, 209, 212
  see also goals; performance

O

opportunity
   see fair wage; mentor; promotion; variety
order 40, 41, 43, 58, 111, 112, 113
organizational charts 46, 165, 186
OSHA 47

P

panic 82, 89, 126
performance
   appraisals 181–188
   measures 144, 209
   objectives 173–181
personal warehouse 20
planning, strategic 124, 204–205
   see also statistical process tools
power 131, 140, 151, 198
power struggles 75
promotion 70, 87, 154
Protestant Work Ethic 229

Q

quality of life 24–27, 36
quotas
   see goals; numbers; performance

R

rankings 181–184, 187
rear view mirror 177
relationships
   see meaningful relationships
religio *216*
restaurant 168–169
rigidity 114, 165–166, 170, 184
Roosevelt, Franklin Deleno 45, 49, 50
rules 52

S

St. Benedict 35, 229
schools 177
Schweiger Industries 49
self-organizing 74, 167, 168
senior people 52
statistical process tools 175
    see also numbers
suggestion box 21
sunglasses 50

T

technology 56, 225
terrorist 108
titles 70–74, 169, 191
track and field 67
    see also athletic terms; coaches
training 71, 87, 107–111, 115, 174, 196
trust 50, 52, 80, 100, 117, 158, 216, 217

V

values, management communicating 19
variety 29–30, 37

W

wages 209
    see also fair wage
watches 211
Weber, Max 20
Wheatley, Margaret 167, 195
Whitney, John 47
wisdom 43, 127, 193, 221

CITATIONS

Many of the quotations in this book were reprinted from *The Manager's Book of Quotations*, Lewis D. Eigan and Jonathan P. Siegel, Copyright 1989, by The Quotidian Corporation. Published by AMACOM, a division of American Management Association International, New York, NY. All rights reserved.

The quotation at the top of the chapter titled *Keep Your Eye On the Prize—The Customer Is Everything*, is used with permission of Robert E. Farrell, author of *Give 'Em The Pickle*.

The quote from Matthew 15:14 at the top of the *"I Don't Have A Clue"* management style is from the New American Bible, Catholic Book Publishing Company, New York, 1970, 1986.

Dictionary definitions are from the *American Heritage Dictionary of the American Language*, copyright 1992, Houghton Mifflin Company.

Thesaurus citations are from *Roget's Thesaurus of English Words and Phrases*, copyright 1962, 1982, 1987, Longman Group UK Limited.

About the Author

Art Bobrowitz has been a passionate student of people and their relationship to work for more than twenty years. Born and raised in Wisconsin, Art spent twenty-three years with the Oregon State Police public safety program. For nineteen of those years, his primary duties were training, media relations, and public speaking. His last eight years with the program were spent teaching at the Oregon Public Safety Academy at Western Oregon University where he was recognized as Instructor of the Year in the Leadership and Supervision program in 1996.

Since then, Art has used his twenty-plus years of management research and experience to launch Compass Rose Consulting, a management and productivity consulting group. He is in high demand as a speaker and trainer and consults with a wide variety of corporations and governmental agencies on productivity, customer satisfaction, communication, goal-setting, and other topics.

Art lives with his wife, Roseann, in Keizer, Oregon. He is active in local government and is a multi-engine commercial pilot.

Bring *Each Human Spirit* to your organization as a presentation. To inquire about workshops, consulting projects, or speaking engagements, contact Art Bobrowitz directly or through the publisher.

Art Bobrowitz
Compass Rose Consulting
Ph. 503.390.6487

Opal Creek Press, LLC
Main Office 503.375.9015
Mary Rowinski, publicity 503.391.5387
Email: authorserv@opalcreekpress.com